Good Can Always Come From Adversity

First Published in 2024 by Echo Books

Echo Books is an imprint of Superscript Publishing Pty Ltd

ABN 76 644 812 395

Registered Office: PO Box 669, Woodend, Victoria, 3442

www.echobooks.com.au

National Library of Australia Cataloguing-in-Publication entry.

Creator: Michael Stein, author.

Title: Good Can Always Come From Adversity

ISBN: 978-1-922603-26-5 (hardback)

NATIONAL LIBRARY OF AUSTRALIA

A catalogue record for this book is available from the National Library of Australia

Book and cover design by Andrew Davies.

echo))
BOOKS

Good Can Always Come From Adversity

The Remarkable Life of Holocaust Survivor George Moshe Stein

Michael Stein

All profits from sales go to the
Queensland Holocaust Museum and Education Centre

This book is dedicated
to the memory of:

Mikosh Stein

Helena Stein

Anita Stein

George Moshe Stein
1st February 1927 – 18th April 2022

Gertrude Stein
17th January 1926 – 30th January 2006

Frank Stein
5th December 1958 – 30th March 2009

Rachel Michelle Stein
5th February 2007

CONTENTS

8

PROLOGUE

Michael Stein

This book is the story of my late father George Moshe Stein, a survivor of Auschwitz-Birkenau and Dora, where he was part of the famous three hundred selected to construct the V-2 rocket in horrid conditions in underground tunnels where at least 40,000 people perished. These rockets caused horrific death and destruction mainly to England. After this he was sent to living hell Bergen-Belsen.

This biography is based on the writings and factual events of my late father, and tells of survival, heartbreak, tears, and determination to overcome all obstacles and build a new life after the devastation of the Holocaust, for himself and his life partner of over sixty years, Gertrude (Trudy) Stein, the love of his life.

The second love my father had was the South Brisbane Synagogue which he rebuilt brick by brick; and yearly visits with Trudy to the memorial service at the museum at Dora, telling the story and educating future generations about the Holocaust (Shoah); and the establishment of a permanent Holocaust Museum in Brisbane, a dream that he never saw come to fruition but became a reality after Dad's passing. It is now open and all of his dreams have been fulfilled.

On his death bed two days before his death, Dad looked at me with a stern expression on his face and said, "I do not want to go yet. There is a lot more that I want to say. Please say it for me".

I promised that I would and I am.

INTRODUCTION

Jason Steinberg,
Chairman,
Queensland Holocaust Museum and Education Centre

On the evening of Thursday 22 October 2020, I approached a man who was a true champion and one of my heroes: 93-year-old Queenslander, Holocaust survivor George Stein. As always he was confident, talkative and carried a commanding presence. With tears in my eyes, we shook hands and celebrated together the news that the Jewish community had just received commitments from all three levels of government funding to establish the state's first Holocaust museum.

This project was a dream George had since July 1982, when he coordinated the first Holocaust exhibition in Queensland. Held at Brisbane's City Hall, under the auspices of the Queensland Jewish Board of Deputies, with then-Premier Sir Joh Bjelke-Petersen as the patron, the exhibition attracted over 10,000 visitors. All visitors participated in Holocaust learning and commemorative activities. George co-ordinated the entire exhibition and involved many other survivors to be involved as guides, deliver lectures, and educate the visitors.

In his own words in October 2020 regarding the importance of having a Queensland Holocaust Museum, George said: "As the number of survivors decreases every year, a memorial to all the victims is very important. For all Queenslanders and visitors to have the opportunity to hear and learn about the Shoah is vital for future generations. We must never forget what happened."

It's hard to imagine the unimaginable things that happened to George during the Shoah. The horrors of concentration camps, the loss of loved ones, and experiencing the depths of human cruelty.

Yet, in the face of such adversity, he emerged as a symbol of hope, dedication, and perseverance for not only our small Jewish community, but also politicians, teachers, students, businesspeople, and the general public. And as the title of this very important book says: good can always come from adversity.

George's survival was not just a matter of chance, it was a testament to his courage and determination. Though the tragic events of the Holocaust could never be erased, George built a beautiful, rich and full life with his wonderful wife Trudy and family, one that was completely devoted to Judaism, Zionism and Holocaust remembrance. When he passed away on 18 April 2022 aged 95, it was George's dedication to these ideals that shone like a beacon to humanity. He worked tirelessly for the Jewish community and to educate future generations about the Holocaust, sharing his own experiences and speaking out against hatred and bigotry.

George was a pillar in the Queensland Jewish community. He was a foundation member of B'nai B'rith, and was president of Brisbane's Chevra Kadisha, State Zionist Council of Queensland and South Brisbane synagogue and vice president of the Jewish Communal Centre of Queensland. He also served on the executive of the Queensland Jewish Board of Deputies and was Vice President of the Zionist Federation of Australia.

In honouring George Stein's memory, so well described in this book by his dedicated son Michael, let us all pledge to continue the work he began – to remember the past, to educate future generations, and to strive for a world where the horrors of the Holocaust are never forgotten and never repeated.

Jason Steinberg
Chairman, Queensland Holocaust Museum
and Education Centre
President, Queensland Jewish Board of Deputies
November 2023

FOREWORD

Greg Cary
Radio 4BC

In my years as a broadcaster on 4BC Brisbane I came to like and respect George Stein enormously. More than that, I admired the passion he brought to the story he dedicated his life to telling.

My stepfather, Kurt Dodge, was Jewish and escaped Austria as a young man after the Anschluss in 1938. Many in his family who remained perished. So I was steeped in knowledge of the Nazis and empathy for their victims. Indeed, throughout my life I have sought greater understanding by reading widely on the subject and speaking to those who knew most about it. People like George.

As the Holocaust and those who survived it recede from modern memory to become part of history, it is both timely and important that Michael recounts his father's journey. It will afford generations to come an opportunity to read a personal account of an evil that still defies our capacity to fully comprehend it. But comprehend it we must, and George dedicated his life to honouring those who died by telling their story at every opportunity. As Michael now tells his.

Antisemitism, of course, was neither confined to Germany nor the times in which it saw its ugliest manifestation. There have always been willing helpers – and still are. Surveys tell us that knowledge of the Holocaust is diminishing, which only makes more possible some version of it happening again. President Truman was right: there is nothing new under the sun except the history we don't know.

This is the important story of one man and the times in which he lived. It is also a powerful account of the history we must all know – and never forget.

Greg Cary
Broadcaster/author
6 October 2023

The day after these words were written Hamas launched its infamous attack on Israel.

Good Can Always Come From Adversity

CHAPTER 1

The Beginning.

George Moshe Stein

Oradea, Hungary (Romania)

I, George Moshe Stein, was born on the 1st February 1927 in the Romanian town of Oradea, 12 kilometres from the Hungarian-Romanian border which in 1920, as a consequence of the treaty of Versailles, ceased to be the Hungarian town of Nagyvárad and became a Romanian town. It had a population of 65,000. The Jewish population made up half of the residents. In older days the area was known as Transylvania. I lived there until 1944. My father, Mikosh (Michael) Stein was a decorated soldier for war service, with the Austro-Hungarian Army in World War I. He was a shoemaker by trade, and president of the local synagogue. He could not anticipate that political developments would one day turn his fellow Hungarians, who spoke the same language, against the Jewish people of this town. The German national socialists would initiate

On their wedding day in 1919, George Stein's parents, Mikosh
and Helena, who perished at Auswitz-Birkenau along with their
daughter Anita.

a policy of ethnic cleansing and genocide throughout
Eastern Europe.

My mother Hawa (Hannah) Stein (née Holzer) was a
seamstress. They married in Nagyvárad in 1919. And I also
had a sister Anita, six years older than me, who worked in an
office. They would all perish in Auschwitz. Life was good
until 1942. I used to play soccer on the cobblestone street
in front of our house with other Jewish friends. I went to
a Romanian Jewish primary school but do not have many
recollections from this period of my youth. Antisemitic
behaviour was not only tolerated by the church but freely

encouraged in Hungary. The government also instigated discriminatory attitudes towards the Jewish people. For instance, Jewish apprentices could only be taught by a Jewish tradesman under the guise of numerous clauses. University places were restricted to prevent the Jews from gaining access to higher education. I received high school education in my hometown and studied Electrical Engineering, for one year at the technical institute, and continued to live in Oradea until 1944; and then had an apprenticeship with a highly qualified Jewish fitter and turner with an excellent and very well-equipped workshop. We had an exceptionally large family. I had cousins, associated relatives; my grandparents on my mother's side had nine children. It was a large and happy family.

All Jews in 1942

Jewish young men were forced to work in the youth brigades digging trenches and foundations. If they missed a day, they were subject to severe punishment and physical abuse. Jewish men of military age (18 to 40) were organized into forced labour brigades in Russia. Before the war, Jews could study in Hungarian universities without being obstructed. Our hope faded quickly when from 1942 the right-wing element of the Hungarian parliament managed to force the implementation of anti-Jewish laws, based on the racist and discriminatory Nuremberg laws. The best Jewish hospital in Budapest used to welcome Jewish patients. Now there were signs erected saying that this was a purely Aryan shop, meaning that the owners and employees of these shops were to be non-Jewish. And Jewish shops were boycotted.

The Nazis know how to intimidate and break people. Up to 1942 Jewish men served in the regular Hungarian Army. They were then disarmed, and all able-bodied men aged from 18 to 45 years old were consolidated as auxiliaries and sent to distant Ukraine, where they had to work, without adequate protection against the climate, and they were grossly abused by the Hungarian guards. This was forced labour at its worst. Jewish doctors were told that they had no value as medical men and were forced to do forced physical work. The Jews had to sleep in tents and barns. The temperature sank down to minus forty degrees. Half of these Jewish auxiliaries were dead by early 1945. Jewish manufacturers suffered extortion and severe restrictions.

My father was in the shoe business, but he received no allocation of leather or a permit to import raw materials. At the same time it was strictly forbidden to lay off workers. Jewish musicians were not allowed to perform in public. They were only allowed to perform in the synagogue. No matter how well you had served Hungary in the past, it was no use now. In World War I many Jews served with distinction in the German Army. When Hitler came to power this military record became irrelevant. Often a Jewish business leader was replaced in Hungary by a dummy administrator who took charge of his business.

The country was now controlled by a puppet of the right-wing regime. Adolf Eichmann came to Budapest to organize the deportation of Jews as their final fate, the so-called 'Final Solution'. Regretfully the Jewish leadership failed us, and they always gave in to the German demands. Our leadership was obviously playing for time, as the ultimate collapse of the Reich was already foreseeable. The infernal plans by Eichmann and the other SS were to destroy the Jewish community of Hungary. Antisemitism has a history going back hundreds of years. When Jewish school children played soccer matches, they could only play with children of other Jewish schools. Jews had to wear the yellow star and so were easily identified as targets. Anti-Jewish propaganda perpetrated by the state was ever present.

We naïvely hoped that by tomorrow things would improve but they did not, they only became worse. By 1944 the Allies had detailed information about the concentration camps and what was happening to our people there. The Allied leaders had difficulties in believing the incredible horror stories that eyewitnesses had reported and confirmed. The Allies thus knew the truth. The reason for this was political, mainly from the United States, for two reasons: 1. it would be unpopular with the people, and they would lose votes; 2. prisoners would be killed, and that would create outrage across the world. Their view was that the camps were of no significance as military targets, and that nothing would be achieved by bombing the targets.

One morning notice was posted in Oradea stating that a total curfew was now in force. All Jews had to assemble in a central place. The gendarmerie and Hungarian police arrived and sealed off our houses and apartments. We thought that we would be able to reclaim our possessions at a later stage. We were allowed one blanket or sheet. Our wedding rings and watches were removed from us. We were then removed from our houses and issued with yellow stars saying 'Jude', and placed in the Ghetto, an enclosed locked area common to restrict Jewish prisoners of the Holocaust. That was the last time that I saw my house until after liberation from Bergen-Belsen.

The Ghetto was a district which was traditionally inhabited by incarcerated Jewish people. It was fenced in by a four-metre-high barbed wall. Wood was in noticeably short supply, as it was needed for the German war effort, but the wood was from provincial Hungary, and we would be held in the Ghetto for a pound, to lock us up, and to keep outsiders from looking in. There were 'no' conditions in the Ghetto, no food, no water, no sanitation facilities, no electricity. We were led to believe that we would be resettled in short time only. We could not imagine that all of us would be deported to Auschwitz. Some of the Jewish leaders from Budapest knew what was happening. They were ensured that their own families could survive. Non-Jewish Hungarians were very willing in helping to round up Jewish people. Under the given conditions, some Jews managed to look after themselves, and survived. Everybody tried to survive. Very few could make deals. The richest industrialist in Hungary was a Jew and was able to go to Portugal. I was naïve. I could have escaped, but instead I listened to others.

We were beaten for the purpose of making us reveal the location of hidden assets. I remember a poor old bootmaker with ten children who was taken to his original workshop. He was eventually tortured because the Nazis thought he had some hidden assets in his workshop. How can you with ten children? We were treated like animals. To humiliate us, the synagogue became the jail in the Ghetto. Jews were also interrogated there for hidden assets.

I managed to get out of the Ghetto several times. At night through the channel of the sewer I crawled out through the manhole on to the street. There were garden beds of vegetables growing in them so I collected what I could carry and managed to bring it back. At a later stage, the Hungarians became aware of this and welded up the sewer covers and dumped tons of sand on top.

The Ghetto consisted of some apartment blocks and houses, of which some were multistorey. You had twenty people in the house. It was easier to keep people together, because of the head count and the control of the people. There was a daily counting procedure, my father was put in charge of the room and was responsible for the correct count, and report that all twenty were here to the Gendarme. The Ghetto was nothing more than a prison and we had no freedom of movement within. We could not observe any Jewish occasions because of the cramped living conditions.

There, even for my father who was deeply religious and president of the synagogue in our town of Oradea, it was absolutely impossible to keep the dietary rules, to keep Sabbath, or any Jewish festivals because the meals were not there, the conditions were not there. Going to the synagogue was impossible because it was used as a prison by the Hungarian Gendarmerie, so it was closed off. Religion was of a low priority except for the day before our deportation. We were told to get ready. Some special prayers and psalms were recited.

CHAPTER 2

The Journey to the Auschwitz Death Camp.

We stayed in the Ghetto for three weeks. Our family was deported with the first transport of people, as it turned out. We were on our way to Auschwitz-Birkenau on the 6th May 1944. We had no idea of this at that time. We were put into cattle wagons according to the pre-existing regulations of the railways. Eight horses or twenty people were fitted into such a wagon. There were one hundred of us. I carried a small eight-month-old baby in a basket.

The non-Jews saw us depart. We could see them through the openings which were covered with barbed wire. Our departure was to their advantage. Some even made the gesture of symbolic execution by sliding fingers across them throats. They were keen to take what we had left behind.

The train journey was a nightmare. There was no food,

no water. Whenever we stopped, we begged for water in the language of that location, as we realized then that the train had left Hungary. We were numbered as a result of the privations. We made a pact and arrangements amongst us all to meet after this ordeal was over in our hometown of Oradea, if we survived after the war. No contact was ever made with any other survivors from this ordeal.

The train arrived in Auschwitz-Birkenau, after travelling in horrendous conditions for three days, at about 3 am in the morning. I cannot explain the experience, it still haunts me. I have difficulties thinking and talking about it. Australia is not far away enough for me to leave this horrible experience behind. We were all trapped! Thirty to forty people per hundred perished.

Birkenau. The Living Hell

We arrived at Birkenau, the extermination camp of Auschwitz. In English Birkenau means 'Meadows of the Birch Trees', but there was nothing poetic about this evil place of death. All Jews marked for death arrived at Birkenau. The instinct of new arrivals told everyone that there was no chance of survival here. Each train bought three thousand Jews and others: gypsies, gays, non-Aryans, and non-believers of the third Reich. The Nazis wanted to destroy them all. A train load was classified as three thousand people.

The Nazi method was to take dignity away from people. Auschwitz was the degradation of human beings.

Everything followed a plan: screaming and the creation of pandemonium, the beatings on arrival. The other Jews told us not to bother about our luggage.

"Where you are going you will have no need for luggage." we were told. We could not function as we were totally exhausted and confused. It felt like Dante's Nine Hells without first going through Purgatory. When daylight broke, I saw a large smoking chimney, then a second and then a third. There were five crematoria. There was a filthy smell of death in the air. We picked up quickly what was in store for us.

You could not even say or wave goodbye to anyone. If you did you would be knocked down and beaten. My mother was carrying a child in her arms and asked if it was hers. She answered "Yes." She was immediately told to go and have a shower – sent to the gas chambers. I never saw her again. My father was also sent to the gas chambers. My 20 year old sister Anita was spared the gas chambers, but passed away two weeks later of typhoid. That was the last time I saw them. I have never gotten over this.

We were called 'Stücke' (meaning lumps or pieces of rubbish). We ceased to be people, living people. This was genocide, without precedent in world history.

I have an English copy of a rare document, the Wannsee Protocol. It is a revised and more accurate translation of the trial 'war on criminals'. It is the transcript of a meeting near Berlin which was chaired by Reinhard Heydrich. It was attended by other leading Nazis and SS leaders such as Adolf Eichmann. This document is the blueprint for a gruesome plan to comb all European countries for the Jewish people from east to west, and north to south. Here are two short extracts:

1"Evacuated Jews will first be sent group by group to so be called transit ghettos, from which they will be transported east".

"Under proper guidance, in the course of the Final Solution, the Jews are to be allocated for appropriate labour in the east. Able bodied Jews, separated according to sex, will be taken in large work columns to these areas for work on roads. In the course of this action, doubtless a large portion will be eliminated by natural causes."

This was how I was separated from my father, mother and sister. I never saw them again.

One of the *kapos* (civilian prisoner guards loyal to the SS, mainly Polish) told me to tell the SS at the selection process that I have a trade qualification and that I am willing to work. I was only 16, but I told them that I was 17 (this was the minimum age). Auschwitz-Birkenau was only a camp for destruction, a 'death camp' of destruction. Nobody was supposed to survive there. It was designed for the mass destruction of people at the height of the Hungarian action. 20,000 people were disposed of in one day. Whilst waiting to be moved the barracks where I was staying, was only two hundred or three hundred meters away from the crematorium and gas chambers. You could see the smoke coming from the chimneys, and it was spoken about by other prisoners who had arrived before me.

Nobody begged for mercy, Jewish people never beg for mercy. It is in their nature not to, and it also was useless as nobody survived the gas chambers when they knew what the situation really was. What did go through their minds? This is extremely hard to explain. But they did accept their fate because it was inevitable – there was no way out. The Jewish people, because of their strong beliefs, character and history, know that they will always overcome adversity. I was once put against the wall by the SS and waited for the bullet to come. You are totally dumb and your mind goes blank. The bullet never came, thank God.

The process for the gas chambers and crematoria went as follows. I cannot tell you what exactly happened because I was not there in person, and I do not like to talk about situations that I have not experienced. Personally, but what I have seen when we arrived, we went through the same process exactly the same clothes, to create a mound of clothes that other people later used. All of our hair was shaved off. We had to go into a dip tank, filled with liquid chlorine, and to submerge ourselves for disinfection purposes. It burnt our eyes and skin. It was undiluted chlorine, it was white. Then a *kapo* held us head under in the chlorinated water. There was a lot of torture and it caused a lot of unpleasantness, created for the pleasure those sadistic *kapos*. It was very unnecessary. There were thousands and thousands of tortures devised. They shaved our heads, armpits, every bit of hair had to be removed to eliminate lice. The *kapos* spoke Yiddish (an ancient language from the ninth century spoken in Europe mainly), and that was accepted because of their Polish origin. The *kapos* told us everything in a very business-like manner, and told us to never give up as they were also Jewish. They were apologizing, "Look, I have nothing to do with this. I am a slave like you are. I am doing this because I have to do it under duress" and so on. "I have to do it. This is the situation".

Above the camp there is an incredibly famous sign, *'Arbeit macht frei'* ('Work makes you free') that was everywhere. We were prey for deceptions, because if they would have put 'Abandon all hope ye who enter here', a quotation from Dante's *Inferno*, it would have been far more appropriate. We did not know what to expect, we did not know what was going to happen. You were not in control of your fate or situation. You just had to switch your mentality completely off, and adapt to that herd instinct, and switch yourself off as an individual, or you would have gone mad. Women were never together with men. There was complete separation, except the Gypsies.

I can say that those prisoners who assisted the prisoners at the unloading at the end at Auschwitz-Birkenau were part of the Sonderkommandos, or part of the group that were working at the disposal and at the crematoria. They told me in Yiddish, "If you want to survive tell them that you are 18 years old and willing to do anything", (I was only 17) "and that you have a trade, that is all you have to tell them". We caught on immediately. We knew what he meant, and those exactly were the questions we were asked at the selection process. We confronted the German officer, who really was employed by Volkswagen Works. We were then put into two lines, left or right.

There was not enough food to sustain you, it was the same thing every day. First, to drink you had a kind of coffee, a bit of a brownish liquid with no taste of coffee at all, and the water had a metallic taste. You could not drink the water out of the tap because it was – I do not know what it was treated with – but drinking the water would have caused a profoundly serious health problem. But nevertheless, if you are thirsty like we were, we still drank it. I am here today. But we were warned not to drink it. The method of eating was that you lined up in lines of five. The one first in line received the pot with the coffee and handed it across his shoulder to the other prisoner behind him. The other one had a sip and handed it back further down the line to the fifth person then he took one sip and handed it over his shoulder. We handed it back to the front again, and everyone was watching that the other one should not take more than one sip. This was the degree of humiliation which is exceedingly difficult to describe because of the value. You received it every day, and the bread I think was made out of sawdust. A terrible process was actually constructed to destroy will and individuality, and to destroy the human spirit. The food was a sort of cruel mess. I do not know what. It was watery, filled your stomach yet had no nutritional taste, but we would still eat it. One loaf the size of a brick was for eight people. You received it every day, and the bread I think was made out of sawdust.

There were no provisions made for physical work in Auschwitz-Birkenau. Auschwitz proper, three kilometres away from Birkenau, was a labour camp where German heavy industries were active, and their main function was the production of industrial chemicals and synthetic rubber 'buna'. They produced sarin nerve gas. They were all set up there, and the prisoners used to work there in horrendous conditions.

We stayed in the barracks for two weeks, five hours a day were taken up by counting. At daybreak, one had to line up outside the barracks – even the dead that died overnight. They were laid down on the ground next to us so that they could be counted and a SS (I would not say a man) came over and counted all of us, including the dead.

We all had numbers in Auschwitz. They were tattoos, done with a special pen, with an allocated number. I got mine, which has been surgically removed, but those marks are still there. All prisoners were marked with the instrument used to inscribe that tattoo. AIDS did not exist at that time; the same pen was used on thousands and thousands of prisoners without even changing it or sterilization. So there was no consideration for hepatitis and this did not bother them in the slightest. Medical treatment was non-existent.

And the other thing was the medical experiments that took place under the control of Dr Josef Mengele. Another thing that I remember: after we got off the rail wagons at Auschwitz, a German soldier screamed out "Are there any Jewish twins amongst you?" If there were twins, or deformed people, they wanted to know, and those people were taken to Dr Mengele's soiled hospital where they were experimented on. They experimented with mass sterilization. With men they experimented with x-ray of the sexual organs. The total aim was to make the undesirable people non-productive and to make them like animals working as their beasts of burden until their strength was gone, to die of sickness or a horrible death, but even the unhealthy ones would not be able to reproduce themselves. This was part of the German theory which they put into practice. There was no such thing as compassion by the *kapos*. It was not in their training as they never ever showed any sign of compassion or pity, none whatsoever. On the contrary, for a German SS guard you are only a beast, not even a chattel. Yes, you are a beast in the person of man, or a name that did not exist as a human being.

There was an exception by a German civilian, a high-ranking Nazi Party official who spoke to us in a civilised manner. When he selected us in Auschwitz-Birkenau for this specialised work, he treated us like people and tried to maintain a sort of civilised approach. He was the only one. He was an engineer from the Volkswagen Works. I even know his name. After I survived, I wanted to visit him many years later, but he had died. He was a lovely fellow. I planted tree on his behalf in Israel to show my gratitude. There were certain civilian workers some of them who exhibited some human feelings – not many but they did. This engineer, who selected us (and me), asked for three hundred specialists, and his actions were very similar to Oskar Schindler, who also rescued many Jewish people in war torn Europe. He could not find three hundred amongst us all, only about two hundred. As he had to make up the numbers, as he was entitled to take three hundred to make up his quota, he pointed at some of the prisoners who were standing next to the barracks there and said, "Come in and join us". Hesitantly they did this. Some were lawyers, some of them were students, others were without qualifications. But he selected, I would say, about one hundred unqualified ones, to make his quota, and he did not subject them to any test.

CHAPTER 3

VW Works Wolfsburg and Peenemünde.

After two weeks of hell at Birkenau, I was selected to be one of the famous three hundred by the German civilian engineers from Volkswagen Works. The Nazis sought and gained financial and technical assistance from many large German corporations.

The test was simple. I was given a slide rule and a metal rod. I had to measure the circumference of the rod. It was simple as I had completed my technical training at Oradea in Electrical Engineering and fitting and turning. He was amazed. I passed and selected immediately. I lied about my age. I said that I was 18 but had just turned 17. Volkswagen Works was in charge of the of the buzz bomb V-1, and later the V-2 rocket project.

Many years later in the United States of America, a class action against Volkswagen Works regarding damages caused by the bombing and death of the population the United Kingdom, and the use of forced labour. I received a lifetime pension payment. I was flown first class to Volkswagen headquarters in Germany along with other Dora survivors and also given other confidential benefits by Volkswagen. They made this gesture as, if word had gotten out that this had occurred, their position in the marketplace and worldwide sales would have been compromised. I departed Auschwitz-Birkenau and I vowed never to return to this hellhole which deprived me of my family, and I never did.

The next was by train to Wolfsburg, in the heart of Germany, where the V-1 rocket was being built and tested. The Germans desperately needed our skills. The accommodation at Volkswagen Works Wolfsburg was not too bad, they provide hot showers, and it was clean. The camp was a part of the factory complex converted to a dormitory, concentration camp style. Each person had their own bunk. The SS were in charge and control was regulated by them. It was completely closed in and an isolated compound. Once more your head was shaven and we had to wear a stripped KZ (*Konzentrationslager*) uniform pyjamas, so even if you would have escaped, you could not take two steps without being immediately caught and returned. That is why the cut hair, the prison uniform and the tattoo: no German civilian would have helped you, and you were in the heart of Germany. The food was better that it was at Auschwitz but not sufficient.

We only had four or five weeks at Volkswagen Works at Wolfsburg, when the British Airforce bombed the complex. Due to espionage the exact location of the factory where the V-1 rockets were built had received a full direct hit. The date was 24th June 1944. I can remember the date very well when the planes came over in force and levelled the factory to the ground. We were locked into our bunkers, and that was an air raid that I will never forget in all of my life. But also an air raid that we secretly cheered. The raid put an end to the Volkswagen Works Wolfsburg.

After the air raid we nearly suffocated because the ventilation system broke down when the electricity stopped working. After five hours the SS opened the steel doors to the bunker, and then let out. Everything was a rubble. It was still burning, and we were let out onto the open space in the meadow. We were guarded until the next day by the SS.

We were loaded onto a transport train and taken to Peenemünde, a complex also managed by Volkswagen Works. This complex was also raided and destroyed by the Royal Air Force who also knew about the complex. Peenemünde was a large establishment, with its own power station, large workshops and refineries for the manufacture of rocket fuel. Accommodation was non-existent. This facility was managed by the well-known Dr Wernher von Braun, a high ranking member of the Nazi party, who was later taken to the United States and forgiven for all of his sins and war crimes. He later established NASA and the United States Space programme. He was welcomed with open arms by the Americans. He is featured in the documentary *Hitler's Engineers*.

CHAPTER 4

KZ-Gedenkstätte Mittelbau-Dora, Nordhausen.

"Dora is such a beautiful name – a girl's name. I don't know where they found it. How could such a lovely countryside be the scene of so many deaths and carnage?" – George Moshe Stein

An extract from *Dora KZ 'Totalen Kriegs' (Dora – Concentration Camp of the 'Total War')*, a film by Loretta Walz.

The season of the year: winter 1944. The month: December. The day: any day of the month. Location: a wooden barracks on top of a hill near the electric fence at the infamous KZ-Gedenkstätte Mittelbau-Dora near Nordhausen, north Germany. The time of day: 6 am.

It is dark outside. Only the yellowish lights on the electric barbed wire fence are visible in a regular square

pattern surrounding the camp. All of this is visible through
the barrack windows, kept open to provide fresh air for
some 150 unwashed, smelly prisoners, some barely visibly
recognisable as the individuals that they were a few months
ago, the frosty air coming through the windows preferable
to the foul one inside the barracks. Our people are lying
half asleep on double-bunks. The mattresses are made of
wood shavings; the only blanket is a louse infested rag;
the pillow is a pair of wooden canvas clogs, with pieces
of electric wire for shoelaces; inside the shoes two pieces
of dark grey triangular rags, cut off illegally from the back
of their shirts to be used as *Fußlappen* (foot rags). To cut
a blanket was sabotage with its consequences. Inside the
foot rag, stuffed into the shoes, was a piece of stale bread
to be eaten with the morning ersatz coffee. The tops of
their bald heads are visible, and so are their unwashed feet
full of infected sores. Full sleep is not possible because
of the constant scratching of their chest and upper legs,
trying to relieve the itching from lice sores. The exhausted
people on the bunks are conditioned and almost sensing
the time for the light to go on and the scream of the
Blockalteste (barrack head): "*Aufstehen*" ("Get up"). The
order is obeyed immediately. A delay invites a swift contact
of heavy boots of their tormentors. There is no room
between the bunks and to use a baton those on the upper
bunks are not so lucky. The time is now 6 am. Our senses
are conditioned to tell the time, even when there are no
clocks in the barracks. No prisoner possesses watches

except for the privileged ones, like the *kapos*, Blockalteste, or Lagerschutz. With the wake up the coughing and sneezing intensifies to a very high crescendo, and it is not smoker's cough. It is chronic bronchitis, or TB, due to the conditions in the tunnel. Washing or cleaning one's teeth is futile exercise because the water at the tap is frozen solid. The temperature outside is −17°C. The dressing routine is a contortion exercise within the confined space.

Between the bunks, firstly tie up with wire the trouser legs at the bottom to limit the flow of freezing cold air to flow up the legs, before the jacket is put on. A prized possession is a sheet of old cement bag paper wrapped around the chest to ensure that somebody heat is maintained. This commodity was obtained by exchange for bread, from the construction commandos (prisoners forced labour workers) in the tunnel. Next the hidden bread came out from the foot rag, and placed into the pocket of the tunnel workers. The foot rag was once again carefully wrapped around the sore foot, so not to create lumps, and last the shoes (clogs) were treated with grease used in the tunnel to make the shoe softer and waterproof. The shoes were put on last because it was agony to put them on and to take the first steps. Before we left the barracks a lukewarm drink of ersatz coffee was distributed, sweetened with saccharine. This was our breakfast with the saved bread from the night before. The order came, *"Alles heraus"*, and we made our way and descended towards the *Appellplatz* (compound used for roll call). It was dark and bitterly cold.

The steps were slippery. There was an easier path, but it was a lot longer.

The March to Work and Return

It was 7 am and the *Appellplatz* started to fill up with the prisoners assembling within their respective work commands. The temperature was −20°C, but it was not difficult to find our regular assembly lot. The Vorarbeiter already was standing there with his shield, similar in size to the Olympic name shield carried by the participating countries before marching at the opening parade except our shield carried the number 103. This was our command number and written on the shield. The *Appellplatz* was brightly lit with powerful floodlights and the watchtower machine guns aimed at us at all times. Four thousand freezing and hungry prisoners assembled together at the same time could be dangerous. The command strength was usually one hundred prisoners. We quietly assembled in rows of five for easy counting. Attention was the order, usually given through the loudspeakers. At the order we quickly ceased moving our arms and marched on the spot to keep up circulation and not freeze. Our *kapos* pre-counted us at this time. If not for our miserable appearance in our striped garments and caps, we really looked like a group assembled for the opening march past at the Olympic Games except for no cheering or waving.

It is now 7:30 am the order comes again *"Achtung! Achtung! Anteneten"* ("Attention! Stand still"). We quickly separate ourselves from the body contact that we use to transfer our body heat to each other's bodies tightly like animals. The smuggling of our arms and the constant non-stopping stamping our feet continued until the SS arrived at our command to count us, without writing down the count on paper for the time record. This did not make sense. Finally, the order to march came at 8 am. The marching band musicians began to play, and the command closest to the gate marched out, through the open gate with the kapo's shouting *"Links zwei drei vier"* and the Lagerschutz was hitting everyone who was out of step. The Vorarbeiter raised the plaque high with the command identification on it. The order was given *"Mütze ab!"* ("Hats off") when we passed the SS at the gate, who again counted the passing pavement. Clip, clop, the flat feet short steps and the knees barely lifting. It was like dragging an invisible chain, in rows of five. The right arm linked through the left arm of your colleague on your right to maintain a straight line for counting by the SS. This sight will always remain with me.

'The March of the Dammed'
There is nothing like it: the command behind us had to step on the spot until signalled by the SS to advance, the SS had to had to make certain that the preceding commands numbers were properly recorded, and now the marching band and the music fell silent. The instruments froze. The only instrument that kept on playing was the bass drum, so the drummer, a big man, stepped out to the

front and started the beat – boom …boom…boom, a sole instrument. The drummer and the SS wore earmuffs for cold protection. This charade lasted all through the winter months and, like on cue, the drum started to beat when our turn came to march past. The distance between the barracks and the tunnel, a ten-minute fast march, to warm ourselves and increase circulation on a rainy day, we could have made it in five minutes. It was no use in rushing it in front of the tunnel, as it was a bottleneck because the SS insisted on counting us again before entering. The road between the camp and tunnel was guarded heavily by the SS and also dogs at all times as we marched in or out.

Arrival time at the tunnel was timed, at 8:30 am and 8:30 pm for the night shift. '*Schichtwechsel*', or changeover, was at 9 am or 9 pm, except for air raid alerts when there was no movement in or out from the tunnel. The procedure reversed but it was simpler: 9 pm assembly in the tunnel; 9:15 pm counting at the exit of the tunnel; 9:30 pm counting at the camp gate. There was no *Appell*, and we were back in our barracks by 10 pm. It was the time then for the daily soup and bread rations. The night slept throughout the day, and the same procedure restarted at 5 pm. We rarely saw daylight or the sun and we never found out which of our colleagues had slept in our bunks whilst we were at work.

KZ-Gedenkstätte Mittelbau-Dora

24,000 prisoners were in this labour camp. When I arrived

there, it was already completed. It was impossible to
describe. Dr Wernher von Braun was also in charge then.
The conditions tunnels were horrendous, without basic
safety, without breathing apparatus or any dry clothing.
It was an underground lake. They had to sleep if they
ever could next to the noise of jackhammers. There
I was put to work again on the same thing I was doing at
Volkswagen Works Wolfsburg and Peenemünde. My job
was to assemble the gyro compasses (guidance systems)
in the nose of the V-2rocket. We were instructed by
Volkswagen Works Civilian Engineers at Wolfsburg, and
Peenemünde. It was precise, highly specialised work, and
I knew it because of my technical training. I knew what
I was doing. The procedure was explained, and checked
and checked.

I had to be precise, but I never pretended that I knew
what I was doing because I was working like a robot
with my intellect switched off, but doing everything as
I pretended outwardly. There was no need to sabotage
anything. I will tell you why, because quality control at
the assembly plant was non-existent. There were so many
components, and when they were assembled nothing really
went with the specifications, and I knew that the rocket
bomb was not going to work. For example, like a rudder
on an aircraft, if it is 5° out of the straight-line, it means
that the target that it is about to go to would be sixty to
eighty kilometres off course. That is why only ten percent
of the rockets launched never reached their destination.

They rather concentrated on quantity and numbers of rockets launched, not the number of British targets that were destroyed as a total goal. That they are working on manufacturing quota was 120 per 24-hour work shift, controlling the quality at such a rate was impossible.

We had a German civilian *Meister* (foreman) who was a very understanding fellow, very decent and called me by my name and not by my number. I called him aside one day and explained to him the facts of the situation. I had them all written down in my work history. I can give you a copy if you want me to. I told him I wrote it in English, and I had to translate it into German for him. When I brought this fact to his attention, to protect myself and other prisoners, and also himself about all the shortcomings and the non-specifications, and about the faulty instruments that we could not adjust, because the adjustments would not respond. He told me, "Look, this is not our business, not my business" and told me to keep my mouth shut if I wanted to live. The management does not take kindly to any advice from the prisoners, or from the staff, or civilian workers. They must cover it all up. It was a private enterprise using slave labour to cover up for all of those deficiencies that screamed of sabotage. He told me, "Do you understand what I mean faults?" They would be taken outside and be hanged immediately and their corpse left on public display on the parade ground in full view so that all could see. A few days later the problem had disappeared, but the faults were never fixed. They wanted to have no problems, according to him, about the short comings. This is the way management protected themselves. I had learned to live with that. There was an underground movement in the camp led by the French prisoners, and they knew what was happening too. If I would have attempted to rectify or suggest rectifications of these faults, I would not be here now.

Many years later I was approached and commissioned by a German university and a German writer who researches this subject. They asked me to write a history about the V-1 and V-2 rockets, and about the special 300 Jewish technicians recruited and about our experiences. I wrote that essay, and forwarded it to Germany. It was published in technical detail.

I have visited Dora over many years. There has been a museum established to remember and pay homage to the survivors and all of those who perished at that hell hole. I used to go on the 15th April to commemorate and partake in the memorial service and to see the remains of that complex of tunnels.

When the Americans liberated us they first took everything out, with the assistance of Dr Wernher von Braun. The United States 4th Army who liberated Dora on the 16th April 1945 could not believe what they had found. They documented this by films and their army rabbi held a special memorial service and recited 'Kaddish', the Jewish Memorial Prayer for the Dead. Even today no one knows, or will ever know, how many of our brothers perished by dropping into the putrid, foul-smelling subterranean lakes in the tunnels. They took everything that they needed. The tunnels were then handed over to the Russians who covered them up. Only four tunnels are left and, according to the agreement reached by the Allied forces, the tunnels should or would not be used ever again for war or armament manufacture.

Now the Museum Authority has dug out a certain underground passage so that visitors can remember. It was not until fifty years later that I entered the same tunnel. It was a very traumatic, unforgettable experience on that first visit back. I found my old workplace where I worked all those years ago. It had not changed. It was as if I was in a time warp. The smell, the cold, and everything else was still the same. I could not believe that I survived this for nearly one year.

Dora was handed back to the present German government in 1990. I had the very memorable opportunity of entering that tunnel with my old friend Prof Dr Jens Christen Wagner, who is now in charge of all European Holocaust museums and served as chairman of the Dora Museum Board for many years. Because of my failing health and the passing of my darling wife Gertrude, I have not visited Dora or the museum as often as I should have. I miss you Dr Wagner, and will always remember our talks and discussions and helping you with your thesis, and sharing the Penfolds Grange wine that I bought you on my visits.

What kept us going at Dora, from depression or killing ourselves, was the will to live and the promise we all made so many years earlier to return home to Oradea and to meet up with all of our fellow survivors. The other motivation was to survive and to tell the world about this historic catastrophe. It did happen. Six million Jewish people are testimony to this occurrence. In the winter of 1944/45 the average temperature at Dora was 17° below zero, so when we went outside, sometimes we could not stand it. What we had to do was to warm ourselves with each other's body heat. So we formed ourselves into groups, into tight circles and like animals, as mentioned earlier, we transferred our heat from one to the other.

Inside the tunnels there were huge ventilators to eliminate dangerous gases, and there were turbines. Not only the deafening noise but they created a huge draft of cold air and the temperature inside was 8°. We were clothed in summer pyjamas and the German *kapos* wore fur coats and fur-lined boots. We did not even have gloves. Somehow we did manage to survive! Look, I cannot define exactly what, but the only thing that you have to do that I can think of in retrospect, I can tell you again is that you switch yourself off completely. Also you switch your intellect off. You do not think that you do not help your comrades. You avoid being a hero and being noticed. Your comrade is not going to help you; it is every man for themselves. Those are the basic rules of your survival. There is very little time for compassion even, though we knew each other very well in our group of three hundred from the same city, and also we were good friends, and all went to the same Jewish school together. There was also no co-operation. If I can gain an inch, it is human instinct to survive. It does not mean that you do bad or vicious things to each other, but the fact is, it is done to me and that it was a chain reaction and that I did the same thing. There was no brotherhood, and there was no, shall I say, common sympathy. If somebody was sick, well just too bad. He had the misfortune to be sick, as I say, you only have to think of yourself. You place yourself into a cocoon and do not try to think, and then you stop thinking about when you are going to be free.

By the end of March 1945, it was decided that production in the tunnel would stop because they could not transport out the completed V-2 rockets that they had stored in the tunnel, practically clogging it completely. The room would be sealed off, and then be blown up and destroyed – with everyone inside it because we had known the secrets of the V-1 and the V-2 rockets; and to protect the local civilian population from us, had we escaped and gained our freedom. Luckily, this event did not eventuate. In the last few hours of the works, two German Air Force trucks arrived and drove into the tunnel, and all those blueprints, plans and certain equipment were placed and loaded onto these trucks. I was ordered to load these trucks. In control of the loading were German officers in civilian leather coats. All the blueprints and documents were then taken out of the tunnel secretly and that was the passport for Dr Wernher von Braun, the Nazi Party engineer, who was spirited off to the United States. He gave himself up later to the United States Army Intelligence. When we saw those trucks leaving the tunnel, and that the entrance was not guarded at all, we all ran outside and evacuated the tunnel. In front of the tunnel the wagons were waiting to take us to another living and dying hell. It was far from over.

Two things that Dora taught me: 1. never ever waste or take bread for granted, it is sacred; 2. in later years, in my own vehicle repair business I refused to work on customers' Volkswagen vehicles.

It was not only Dora, but in a 50 kilometre radius there were 35 sub-camps of Dora, where the living and working conditions were horrific, the largest being Ellrich sub-camp where mass graves were found after liberation by the First Armed Division of the United States Third Army, and the survivors were transported by rail to Bergen-Belsen.

CHAPTER 5

Living Hell then finally Liberation.

We were ordered onto the wagons, Jews and Russians. We had a better chance of surviving than those that were left behind. It was an unlikely combination as the Russians hated the Jewish people even more than the Germans. It took us five days to arrive at Bergen–Belsen. For five days the wagons were not opened. We were not given any food or water. That was the longest hunger that I have ever known. By the time we arrived at Bergen–Belsen, we had to slide of the rail wagons as we were unable to stand up.

German soldiers and some older guards (over fifty) opened the doors. Nothing really could have been done with the four or five hundred people but to march them into the camp. Bergen–Belsen was located a short distance away in a small forest. We laid down on the ground and just waited to die. We were infested with typhoid and diarrhoea, and all different types of sicknesses that were impossible to describe. This can be seen on the British

Army documentary filmed on the 15th April 1945.

Many years later I was invited by the British Broadcasting Corporation to do a documentary, which I agreed to. You can watch it, but you have to have a very strong stomach as it is horrific. It was strange as the film was made at the time of liberation, but it was not shown and kept under embargo under lock and key for over forty years, so as not to upset the Germans.

We were liberated by the British Forces on the 15th April 1945. What I can remember about my day of liberation was very hazy at the time, to the extent that I was not a human being anymore, and I was not aware that I had been liberated, armed with my empty soup container – it had been empty for many days. My feet were wrapped in rags. I started to wonder around the camp aimlessly in search of something, nothing special. My behaviour was very erratic, similar to those people who wander around in Africa or elsewhere, dying of hunger. So well-illustrated nowadays in television coverage of famines, the relentless feeling of hunger had passed a long time ago. I must have resembled a sleepwalker in broad daylight.

As I dragged myself, I noticed before me that a group of trees were not too far away, like an oasis in a desert somehow. I reached this small forest, and it was very real, not a hallucination. The scene awaiting me in that forest is very impossible to describe, and you have to visualize it in your mind: hundreds of people were standing there embracing the trees for support, trying to reach the lower branches to tear off some leaves for moisture. Water supplies had been cut off in the camp for some time. I tried to do likewise, but I was pushed away. It was like a scene from Dante's *Inferno*.

Being early spring in Europe that did not help me either as deciduous trees are bare until the middle of May. Even Nature was against us all. Towards the evening my legs could not support me any longer and I sat down under the tree, using it as a back support. I shared the tree with some others. I reached for another tree but the branches there had already been picked bare. I was unaware of the fact that the British advance troops already had entered the camp, and that we were liberated; and also that the SS guards had escaped but were recaptured in the nearby vicinity of the camp. From a distance I could hear a brass band playing some lively music, but I could not define if it was earthly or heavenly. I was told later that it was Dora's brass band marching to greet the liberators. I must have fallen into a deep coma or lost consciousness, for how long I do not know – one day, a night, two days, maybe – but I suddenly heard some strange voices and also a strange language spoken out very loudly. I opened my eyes and must have moved or made a sound. It was broad daylight what I experienced was the following.

One of the huge creatures with masks, long rubber gloves and strange camouflage outfit yelled out in an excited voice, "One of them is moving, and awake". I was lying on top and next to dead people. One of the creatures grabbed me and put me on a stretcher. I tried to resist. As fate would have it, one of these British soldiers was a fellow by the name of Morrie Singer. He was Jewish. Many years later, he moved to Brisbane, Australia where I now reside, himself, his wife Grace and children Alan, Peter and Steven, became lifelong friends with all of us.

It was a bad nightmare that had occurred but as it turned out that those saviour angels did save me. They were members of the British Medical Corps. I will always be grateful to Morrie Singer and the rest of these soldiers. They were searching for signs of life amongst the corpses scattered among the trees when they found me. This must have been an Act of God. I was put in the back of a green army truck, with a green canvas top and driven a short distance to a building which was converted to a field hospital. I was put on a wooden table, stripped, and given some sort of injection that I did not feel, and a pill with a drink that I could not swallow. Next, after cutting off my old rags, some sanitary people with white rubber aprons and gloves started to pour warm water all over me whilst scrubbing at the same time. The water must have contained some disinfectant like carbon because it fiercely burned the open, infected sores on my chest, caused by lice infestation of my emaciated body. A liberal sprinkling of white DDT powder followed. I was then put into a white sterile bed, with a tube in my nose. For the first time in nearly two years I slept peacefully without the ever-present need to scratch the sores on my chest. The DDT had done it's work very fast. Sometime later I was spoon-fed with soft yellow custard, which I could not feel the taste – my taste sense did not work – but I could swallow vitamin pills. Two weeks later, and with my typhus infection gone, I was able to walk unaided and eat light solid food, the first slice of white bread was the first that I had tasted in years. Since then it has become an obsession with me, and I will not tolerate the wastage of a single slice of bread in my household.

Four weeks after my miraculous survival I left the hospital in much better shape than a mere skeleton thanks to the devotion of the British Medical Corps and the British Red Cross. I was literally born again, the woods where I was found and rescued was filmed by the British Army, along with the hundreds of unfortunate Jewish and other people that did not survive. This film has been seen many times as documentaries all around the world to show the horrors of Bergen-Belsen.

Our Life in Bergen-Belsen after Liberation.

Life in Bergen-Belsen after the liberation and reoccupation was an enjoyable one. The Jewish survivors, about 15,000 of us, organized our own administration, establishing a post office, and cultural and other educational activities, including English language courses. The British Army chaplain orthodox rabbi conducted religious services. Zionist activities were introduced by emissaries from the Jewish Agency. Food supplies were good and accommodation facilities were satisfactory. The only upsetting matter was the lack of movement outside the camp. No official explanation was given by the British military authorities for the restriction of movement, but we were later found out it was for political reasons: liberated prisoners of France, Belgium, and Dutch origin were repatriated to their respective countries one or two days after liberation, but the Jews remained a problem for the British Foreign Office. In line with the white paper policy, our chances to immigrate to Palestine (Israel) had to be prevented at all costs. We were classified as citizens of an enemy country, like Hungary or Romania, and to be returned to these countries, from where we were originally deported from as Jewish. Those countries revoked our citizenships at the time of deportation, and those countries were now under Soviet occupation. At that time all those facts were not taken into consideration.

This solution was not acceptable to us as we were people without nationality under international law. The plan finally could not be implemented by the British, because in September 1945 the UNRRO (the United Nations Relief and Refuge Organization) took over the administration and control of all refugee camps within the western zones of Germany and Austria under the UN charter. We were finally registered and attained the official status of DP or (displaced persons). Forceful repatriation was not a worry for us anymore, and the registration card issued to us by the UNRRO, enabled us to move around with more freedom, with the exclusion of port cities like Hamburg, for obvious reasons.

Unfortunately at a later stage, in 1947 or 1948, the DP status was greatly misused by escapees from the Baltic states and the Ukraine – some of them war criminals – to gain admission to UN refugee camps in the west and facilitate their speedy immigration to different countries, Australia included, without their wartime background and activities being checked.

Bergen–Belsen was liquidated as a DP camp towards the end of 1945. Because of the lack of opportunities to immigrate from there to other destinations, people moved voluntarily to the United States zone of Germany or to Italy where there were better possibilities to emigrate. The solid buildings within the camp are now the headquarters of the British North Atlantic Treaty Organization (NATO) forces for Europe and a missile base. The part of the camp where the 40,000 fellow prisoners who did not survive now rest in mass graves. It is preserved as a memorial and documentation centre.

I visited there in 1984 and again in 1985.

The Grey Area. Keeping the Promise. Returning Home. The Heartbreak.

I will now continue with another phase of my life which I will describe as a grey area, because not much is known or spoken or written about. For survivors this era represented a turning point in our lives.

Early in September 1945 we, together with a young group of Jewish survivors who came from the same Oradea hometown vicinity in Hungary (now Romania), returned to our hometown. In the rail wagons taking us all to Auschwitz-Birkenau, we had made a solemn promise to our past parents and families that if we did survive, we would one day make this journey home. For obvious reasons, as above, and with a great sense of adventure, we took on this enormous challenge. Our group of ten, nine boys and one girl (the sister of one of the boys), decided to embark on this 3,000 kilometre odyssey to the east. We were warned about the dangers of travelling through war-torn Europe, devastated borders and, what is more, we did not have any documentation or travel permits. We knew the risks involved, and we were all prepared to take them. It turned out to be the best adventure of our short lives.

We prepared ourselves with sufficient provisions and strong boots, and clothing unobtainable outside the camp. We mapped out a tentative route, from an old map that we found, right to the Hungarian border, the rest would be easy as we only lived ten kilometres from there. We discovered that national borders did not exist anymore, only military lines and occupational zones. There was no road transport, only military. The only train was coal transport wagons – the only lifeline with cities in total ruin and devastation. Highways and exits were blocked by military checkpoints to prevent the local inhabitants from moving around and scavenging the countryside. There was no civilian administration and only military government, public order being maintained by the military police. We headed into the chaos with youthful determination and overconfidence.

We also had to learn how to behave towards the German population in real life. On the roads and cities there were signs posted saying, "Do not fraternize or accept food or ice cream from the civilian population by order of the military government". As our journey progressed, our hatred of the German people turned into cold sympathy when passing endless masses of people waiting in line for distribution of bread. We could not allow ourselves to make snide remarks or exhibit signs of hatred towards them. On our first day out of Belsen, we went to a small and most beautiful town on a riverbank with medieval architecture, and a very hospitable population greeted us. You could not imagine my euphoria walking the ancient cobblestone narrow streets of that tranquil medieval city that was undamaged by the war, and the irony was that this city was only 15 kilometres distant from the horror of Bergen-Belsen.

George Stein
Celle, June 1945

I even had my first haircut in a proper barber's chair with a snow-white sheet around my collar and a photo taken at a professional photo shop, which even today is in my possession. The name of this city is Celle. Its citizens friendly behaviour paid off later in the 1980s. Many survivors returned later in their lives with their families to revisit Belsen as a pilgrimage. I did the same. The city built specialist tourist accommodation by converting farmhouses into luxurious hotels for these solemn visitors. There was no music or dancing in these hotels.

Now let me return to my subject. The next day whilst

sightseeing, we were spoken to 'quietly' by some British military police advising us politely to return to Belsen after our day of sightseeing. They did not see our oversize backpacks.

Early next morning we headed for the large city of Hanover, and out of the reach of the British. There was nothing to see there. Being a large industrial city, it was in total ruin. We headed south to Kassel, a city in no better shape than Hanover, on top of a slow-moving coal train. After a good rest in that city, we boarded another slow coal train heading to Frankfurt, but this time we travelled in relative luxury in some empty freight wagons that were attached to the train, and in spite of our aversion and justified hatred of such wagons, we climbed on – but kept the two side doors wide open. We mainly sat in the door openings, giving the impression that the wagon was full and to prevent people jumping in at slow speeds or at stations. We also took care to travel by daylight for our security, but this was not a problem as trains only travelled by day because of signal and track problems.

We arrived four days later at a railway siding which was once Nuremberg's famous glass-covered railway station, and promptly taken guarded by stone-faced military police to the headquarters of the American military government. This was once a luxury hotel and miraculously undamaged by the air raids. We were given proper rooms, not cells, and given dinner at the restaurant under guard. The next morning our interrogation began by a United States security officer: "Who are we? What language do you speak? Where do you come from? What army unit are you a part of? Where are you going to without any papers?"

He left and sometime later a high-ranking United States officer entered the room. We became really very scared. He held a sheet of paper in his hands – it must have been the interrogations report. "I see that you all speak Yiddish and Hungarian. Very good," he began in perfect Yiddish: "I am Colonel Emmanuel Kate of the United States Army and in command of the detachment of the military government," then told us that he was Jewish.

What followed was similar to the scene from *Genesis* 45:1, where Joseph reveals his identity to his brothers. We fell all over him like a long lost relative whilst we were all speaking at the same time to tell him our life stories, and showing him our tattoos and trying to explain the reason for our presence there. After we had quietened down, he explained that he was a lawyer from New York and had enlisted as a military administrator with international legal experience. He heard and knew about the liberated KZ camps, but he had never met a Jewish survivor or had ever visited a camp. You could see by his expression and tone of voice that he was very emotional. By the way, he told us, the first interrogating officer was also Jewish. He stated that he had a good idea of who we were but he wanted to convince himself. He outlined a plan for us and a way in which he would be able to help us. We were advised by him not to head towards Austria because the British,

French and a large Russian presence was there, and the permit that he was going to issue to us would not be valid in that occupied zone. He issued us with a travel permit. It read "To whom it may concern", my name, and another nine young, liberated persons, that they are permitted to travel to Pilsen, Czechoslovakia without hindrance. That was as far as his authority reached, because Pilsen was the last outpost under his control. He also stipulated that route must be via Regensburg, where there was another Jewish officer whom he was friends with, and that he would advise him that we were going there. He offered us further hospitality and a military escort to Regensburg. We thanked him with tears and emotion in our eyes, but with typical hutzpah, in possession of much needed and appreciated travel passes. We will never ever forget him.

We decided to explore the most interesting and historical locations in Bavaria and surrounds, we were given a lift to the nearest undamaged cultural city of Fürth, with its cathedrals theatres, cinemas, and empty shops. As in any large, occupied city, a Judische Kommittee or Jewish welfare organization was established by a group of liberated ex-KZ prisoners. They occupied large houses belonging to former Nazis. They were supplied by provisions by the AJDC (American Jewish Joint Distribution Committee) with the sole purpose of accommodating returning liberated Jewish KZ inmates in those 'safe houses'. The reception by our fellow survivors was very brotherly. We could stay as long as we wanted to. It was like a youth hostel 'proper 1945 style'.

From then we found that almost in every German city in the American Zone, the army's public government administration was under the control of Jewish ranking offices who had legal and organizational skills. It was ironic that Jewish administrators had ruled over defeated Germany's civilian administration. Those safe houses were later utilised as transit centres to accommodate the huge exodus from eastern Europe, later in 1946 and 1947, of Jews who survived the war in Siberia or other Eastern countries, and Jewish partisans. This rescue operation, of which I became an operative member was run and organized by the Bracha ('Escape') Jewish secret organization with great determination and courage until the curtain fell.

After we had enough of sightseeing and visiting the famous winter resorts, we decided to head to our intended final destination, discarding the idea of staying in Germany as displaced persons or involving ourselves in the aspirations of the thriving black market. That idea did not appeal to me. As there had been a dispute amongst us about this subject, I reminded the group about the specific numbers on our travel permits and documents and the ultimate purpose of our undertaking which had to be honoured. The group did not end up splitting. Avoiding East Germany we arrived at Pilsen at the end of September one month after we started our odyssey. In Pilsen we were once again looked after and welcomed by the then reestablished Jewish community.

They briefed us about conditions in Hungary and Romania, and were also able to provide us with an incomplete list of survivors from our home towns. For obvious reasons not to elevate our expectations, we did not want to see that list. The community also provided us with train tickets for Budapest, only a two-hour train ride, but first we decided whilst there in Pilsen to visit Prague for a few days, just to delay the inevitable.

Concentration Camp Syndrome Returns

In Prague one of our group came down with a severe case of diphtheria and we had to leave him in good care in a proper hospital. I met up with him two weeks later in our hometown of Oradea. On our train trip to Budapest we all became victims of severe depression. Our brotherhood fallen had apart. We insulted each other, and concentration camp syndrome had taken over.

The treasured travel document became a useless piece of paper. This was a psychological effect due to our metal state, and I was not quite ready to meet the unexpected situation that was waiting for me at home, with all its memories, good or bad. In fact it was not my home anymore, only a reminder of my tragedy, and the loss of my father, mother and sister.

I arrived at Budapest on the first day of October 1945 and was met at the railway station by members and representatives of the Jewish community. The next day I met some friends who had just returned from home, and they confirmed positively my worst fears, in a very casual and matter of fact manner. There was no room for personal compassion in those times. I had a strong urge to turn back towards the west right there and then. The train journey only being three hours away from Budapest, but when I was on that train, I had wanted the journey to last forever.

CHAPTER 7

Oradea Heartbreak.

On arrival at Oradea, I became completely detached from my surroundings. It was as if I was in a strange planet. But I finally made it home. I walked along the cobbled streets, past the synagogue where we prayed as a complete family and my dear father was proudly the president for many years, traditions passed on to him from his father; past my old school, where I had enjoyed many happy times playing with my friends; then down to my street, Strada Arany János, where again I played soccer with my friends. I found my house, opened the front door of the building, which comprised of six two-bedroom single story duplexes, and went in. Suddenly my mood changed to a feel of relief and joy: finally I was home.

I knocked on the door with vigour and excitement. It then was opened by a huge, burly Russian man. I said to him "I am here. I am finally home after all that I have been through". He cursed at me in Russian and told me to go away. "It is my house now," he told me. After we were removed from our houses and placed in the Ghetto, the non-Jewish population took over possession of the Jews' property and assets, Oradea was under Russian control. My mood changed to one of sadness. Immediately I was devastated, it felt as if a knife had been inserted into me and that my throat had been cut, and that my world had ended right there on the spot. I immediately left and have never been back.

Many years later in 2014, my second son Michael and his wife Karen did the same journey, visiting the museum at Dora, and were greeted by my old friend Professor Dr Jens Christan Wagner, who I met on my first visit there in 1990 after the unification of East and West Germany. He was the first director of the museum when it opened. He is now the director of all Holocaust museums and memorials in Europe. I assisted him with his thesis, and we became the best of friends. I visited yearly for the memorial service in April and have stayed in contact. He is like a son to me. I told Michael that every time that I used to visit I would take two bottles of Grange Hermitage Australian wines as a present. He too did that. They were escorted by Dr Wagner to a private tour of the tunnel and museum, the same as we had done on my first visit. He even showed them my workstation of so many years ago. This tour was very special, as tours are usually only conducted in groups reserved for very important people heads of state and royalty. I gave Michael directions, photos of the house

George Moshe Stein's house, Oradea, Romania

which I still have. They went to Oradea and found my old house. On arrival they were greeted by a young couple who are the present residents. They showed them around the house. Michael took photos and rang and told me. I burst into tears. At the same time the confirmation of the loss of my parents and sister were confirmed – these records are kept at Yad Vashem, the World Holocaust Remembrance Center, in Jerusalem. The other thing that I did was to confirm to myself forever of my town of birth, Oradea, and I renamed it 'town of which was'. I erased it completely out of my mind.

From the 50,000 Jewish people deported from the Ghetto only handful, about three hundred and fifty returned. The Jewish institutions were deserted, empty and looted. The local non-Jewish population took possession of our houses and properties. The city was handed to Russian control so that the new occupier of our house, for example, was Russian.

On the day that the last transport from the Ghetto left for Auschwitz-Birkenau, all this took place with the consent and approval of the government authorities, as a due reward for the local civilians full co-operation with our deportations. Since none of us were ever expected to return, the possession of our properties became permanent according to their law. On our return we had no rights to reclaim. The former fascsist city functionaries were still in power as loyal supporters of the new communist regime.

The now-empty former hospital served as a hostel for us unwelcome returnees. Food supplies were provided by the joint distribution committee but ninety percent of it was stolen on the way from Bucharest to the capitol. After two weeks I decided that my fact-finding mission was accomplished and began earnestly to consider my future action. Since I fulfilled my pledge and obligations, I found myself alone in this big world, under those tragic circumstances. I was free to act on my own behalf and decided to make a new start in my life, but under no circumstances would it be in Eastern Europe under a Communist regime. 'Head west, young man' was my intuition and decision.

I made immediately made contact with the group who returned with me from Bergen-Belsen, and with some others who had the same concern. We agreed that there was to be no future for us here, especially when others and myself in our age group received notifications to present ourselves for military service in the rag-tag Romanian army. This prospect did not appeal to me or to the others. Since my citizenship status was unclear, and my physical strength was not at the required level – neither was my age, short of being 18 – I received a deferral. This gave me the opportunity to arrange escape before I was hunted down and be classified as a deserter.

I discovered that a well-organized underground Zionist organisation operated in the town headed by one of my ex-schoolteachers who had known me since my early childhood. This local organisation was to later be responsible for arranging transit for thousands of Jewish refugees who had survived the war in Siberia as partisans or far away beyond the reach of the invading Nazis. I joined this Zionist organisation immediately and soon became one of their operators, based on my experiences and exploits within the organisation, and it enables me to describe to you their operational methods under which the organization operated. First as a matter of great urgency we were quickly transported overnight across the Romanian border.

Underground Bricha.

The code name for our underground organisation was 'Bricha' (or 'Escape' in Hebrew). Its original organizers and operators were active Jewish officers in the Red Army, and they were joined later by ex-Jewish partisans from the Eastern Front. The language of communications was pure Yiddish. The partisans realised early that they could not trust their family's future to the increasing antisemitic regime of the Soviet Union after the defeat of the Nazis.

Those officers at great personal risk for themselves organised the transport in Budapest the capitol, through the Astro-Hungarian border. They knew exactly the positions of the border posts and the Russian sentries co-ordinating our transport. Accordingly we never came across a border patrol, but at a given location, a rucksack of vodka bottles was deposited by the crossing. On the next night they were gone.

This arrangement worked like magic for all concerned.

Our guides never crossed the Austrian border for their own safety. About two hundred metres after the group cleared the forest, a head count was carried out to make certain that nobody became lost in the thick forest. The strength of our group was a manageable number of forty. The guide then pointed the group to the direction where the two trucks were waiting, well inside the British zone of Austria. I worked that border territory for nine months as a responsible transport officer right under the noses of the British Field Security Service.

From our side of the border our western operations took over. I drove in total darkness on cross-country tracks. Since I only had two trucks at my disposal, it explains the limits of the groups. I used British military trucks with UNRRA registrations. The military police were enforcing a strict military rule – twenty persons per vehicle.

I transported to the regional capital of Graz where we maintained a large share house, for resting and as a transit centre. Our affiliations with the British administration were good and very cordial with the understanding that the refugees as displaced persons would remain in the confined allocated camps and that they would not engage in any illegal or terrorist activities.

I was once taken in for interrogation by the Field Security Services, and asked if I was a Zionist activist, and if I was aware of the fact that illegal immigration to Palestine (Israel) was strictly prohibited by British law, my reply was 'Yes', and that we would wait patiently without

demonstrations within our camps until we could enter
Palestine legally or immigrate to somewhere else. My
frank answers satisfied them, and they turned a blind eye
towards our border crossing activities. The fact that the
average ages of our group was 18 to 40 also escaped their
attention.

CHAPTER 8

A Giant Step to Escape and to Make 'Aliyah'.

The screening for prospective candidates was carried out in Budapest. It was carried out according to a set of strict procedures personally carried out by our Russian operatives. There was a thorough identity and past history check on the individual. Proof of being Jewish was required, and past Zionist activities were also taken into account, also a verbal undertaking was required to make 'Aliyah' (Hebrew meaning 'to ascend or going up') and to settle in Eretz Israel (Palestine) at the earliest opportunity. Also there was a mandatory stay at our designated holding centre, which was the former Jewish high school building in Budapest.

Transport groups were informed only one hour before their departures, always from a different security location and only known to the group leader. As mentioned before, the age bracket was a strictly observed 18 to 40 years old. The reason for this was there a 15 kilometre stretch of forest at the border to be negotiated at a near running step. Unfit persons posed horrific problems to us all.

The other great danger was the possibility of deserters from the occupation forces of the Red Army who might infiltrate our groups and put our organization at great risk by betraying us to the KGB. This rescue operation lasted until the early winter of 1946 when, due to very harsh weather conditions and deep snow, it had to be abandoned. Footprints in the snow can be discovered and followed. The Russians became very suspicious of our activities and it was time to wrap up our operations from Budapest.At the same time our Russian organizers received information from their secret source that the Russians were erecting fortifications and barbed wire fences on the Astro-Hungarian border. This action was not specifically taken to prevent our escape, but to fend of a mass exodus from other eastern nationals and Hungarians, anticipated to take place in the spring of 1947, to escape the ever tightening communist rule.

The last group to leave Budapest was a very special and distinguished one. It was made up of entirely from operatives and functionaries of the escape movement. They had carried with them all the confidential information and records. When they reached the border another small group had joined them.You may be able to guess who they were: they were the six Red Army officers, the backbone of our organization. They had planned their escape very carefully in advance. Only one day, before the borders were totally closed, but not before they made certain that their families were safely across the border with earlier groups. I personally handed them the letters from their loved ones, confirming them of their safety. When I met them all at the border I had onboard a supply of civilian outfits, which they changed into very quickly out of their officers uniforms, and we then buried these in the forest with haste and without a trace, but they kept all their papers and pistols.

As a precaution I sprinted some 250 kilometres away, driving in total darkness again into the relative safety of the American Zone of Germany, as Austria was unsafe for them. They were later reunited with their families in our large Jewish displaced persons camp in Munich, and then onto Bavaria where they registered in their Jewish names.

All together 20,000 Jewish refugees and camp survivors who were liberated by the Russians in January 1945, and others who had survived Romania, crossed those borders safely, thanks to the bravery, dedication and organizational skills, and the Zionist idealism. With a huge personal risk, they helped those survivors and themselves to take the giant step towards a better life and to secure a future for themselves and their families and their future generations. I did meet up with a lot of them later while I was serving in the Israeli Army with my wife Gertrude.

CHAPTER 9

Admont: Peace and Tranquillity.

Admont a picturesque small town in the Austrian Alps. Peaceful, it was in the British zone, surrounded by high snow-capped mountains. At that time there wasn't any rail connection, only a steep, narrow, winding gravel track, connecting the town to the rest of the country. The village was a winter resort before World War Two and only had about 500 inhabitants. The camp consisted of some twenty well-built wooden barracks, with a large kitchen, bathhouse, healthcare facilities and, most important, a very large lock-up garage for twelve trucks to protect them from the snow and frost. It served as a German training facility for winter warfare.

There was only one major problem: the camp was occupied by some 300 Croatian Ustaše Nazi collaborators and their families awaiting immigration processing by their sponsors: the Vatican. They lived on Vatican-supplied 'care parcels'. We had devised a strategy to make them vacate the camp in a great hurry: we simply claimed that we had files on them from Yugoslavian authorities. Since the Russian zone border was only 20 kilometres away, it represented no problem to return them to Yugoslavia and to face swift justice. Of course this was only a bluff but it worked perfectly.

The same convoy of our trucks which transported our first Jewish occupants to that camp was used to transport those Croatians, and their care parcels included, to the Astro-Italian border town of Villach, where they crossed legally to Italy with the assistance of Vatican officials. We were blessed with a windfall profit at the border. The Italian customs would not allow those parcels, and we ended up bringing them back to our camp at Admont! They were literally 'God sent'.

It took us over a week to receive our first supply of provisions from the joint warehouse at Linz. The next step was our approach to the UNRRA (United Nations Refugee Relief Authority) Commission in Austria to appoint a director and official administrators to the camp. After they inspected the facilities, approval was given, but not before we had rigged the head count to qualify for a status as a UNRRA displaced persons camp, Administration Team Five Admont.

CHAPTER 10

Helping the Nazi Hunter.

The Admont camp was a unique institution in itself. It was run by a democratically elected committee representing the four Zionist factions, active in the camp. This system worked very well and harmoniously. The chairmanship of the committee was rotated quarterly. There was an *Arbeitsamt* (Labour Office) which allocated the people to perform the required work to maintain the proper running of the camp. Simply, if you did not do any of the camp work you did not receive the joint food supplement. There was a communal kitchen for single people, but families were provided for independently so that they could look after their own needs. Also there were cultural activities: an orchestra, Yiddish theatre, synagogue, and a school, with the establishment of a medical centre under the supervision of an American UNRRA doctor. The structure was now complete. The two Jewish refugee doctors in the camp could not practice under the current law, but only under supervision of the UNRRA doctor. The surgery also provided free medical services for the town's population.

Our biggest asset was our transport infrastructure. The UNRRA arranged for the transfer of twelve ex-British Army four-ton trucks, and an all-weather ambulance from the British Army surplus depot, with the rights to obtain unlimited fuel supplies.

The ambulance provided 24-hour emergency services to the townspeople also. The nearest hospital was 60 kilometres from the camp. The UNRRA administrators were absolutely marvellous. The camp director was a British officer by the name of Frank Hunt. I had a solid friendship with him, and he became an ardent Zionist supporter. He helped us immensely with our illegal transports. My eight drivers and I were issued with a yellow UN passport allowing free movement within the occupational zones of Austria, except for the Russian zone. This was a great asset because we received all of our supplies from the Linz warehouse of the Joint Distribution Committee once a week for the 3,000 floating residents of our camp.

The operation system consisted of 40 refugees at a time on our two trucks leaving for the American Zone overnight and returning the next day. We would return to Admont loaded with eight tonnes of supplies. In winter, because of the snow, we could not use the mountain back road. We had to use the highway. We could not transport refugees as a result of these activities. I was away from camp 80 per cent of the time. I thoroughly enjoyed these adventures immensely and met some interesting people on those occasions.

In April 1947 I was handed a note from our committee chairman with an address in Linz. On my return trip with our weekly supplies, I had to pick up an unnamed gentleman and bring him back to Admont in secret. I had wondered who the gentleman could be. As it turned out it was none other than Simon Wiesenthal, the famous Nazi war criminal hunter. He was very grateful for the lift and assistance with the transport. He told me that he always chose to travel alone. That was the most interesting 200 kilometres of my life, that I will also never forget.

We spoke and I told him about my experiences so far in my short life: about Auschwitz-Birkenau, Dora and Bergen-Belsen. You could see by looking at his sad, teary face that he was horrified. He then told me his only goal in life is to seek justice for me and also for millions of Jewish people who had died or suffered, and that he would hunt all of these war criminals down no matter how long it took. He also told me that he was not worried or concerned about his safety, as he had put measures in place to look after that.

He then asked me about my duties at Admont. In fact, he was very well-informed about our operations. But one thing that he did not tell me at the time was the purpose of his visit. He did ask for my further help to provide him with a suitable unmarked civilian motor vehicle so that he could undertake and complete his mission successfully.

With some difficulties this was able to be achieved. When this did happen, Wiesenthal made the following request to the chairman of our committee: to ask the services of two strong and reliable individuals, the chairman himself, and he wanted me as his driver to carry out the most important mission of his life.

Preparations were made in the greatest possible speed and upmost secrecy, without disclosing the identity of the intended target or of the mission. This added more significance to the case, and also as he never discussed field work with anyone. The target was some 20 kilometres distance away from our camp. We left exactly as planned at 2 am in the morning. I was very familiar with the country dirt road leading to the location which was on the outskirts of the town of Steyer. Halfway to the target Wiesenthal named the person who was about to be apprehended and taken as our prisoner. It was Adolf Eichmann!

I immediately stopped our vehicle, then the two strong men, ex-partisans, in the car with us questioned the action. "This is not the forest," they shouted, and if able to complete this action it would be kidnapping. The decision was made to take him without harm, then convey him to the regional capital city of Graz and then hand him over to the British Military Administration as a war criminal.

I remarked at that stage that Graz is 200 kilometres away and, as I had not been informed about this plan, that I had not made any arrangements or provisions for the extra fuel that would be required; and also the fact that we were in a civilian vehicle, and we could not obtain fuel from military sources on the way to the target. The first night's mission was then aborted immediately.

We went again the next night and I hid the car some distance away. We almost reached the house when all hell broke loose from the neighbourhood dogs. We then entered the house and found an old woman frightened to death thinking that we were Russian marauders that were trying to rape her. There was no sign of Eichmann and we made a hasty retreat, as history would tell you. He was captured many years later in Argentina. After this exciting episode was over, we returned to normal life in our camp. Over the years I have remained in contact with the amazing Simon Wiesenthal.

With the Austrian elections around the corner, it would mean the return to civil administration and the termination of military operations. The writing was on the wall that gradually all displaced persons camps within Austria would be disbanded and closed, and its inhabitants would be transferred to Germany or Italy. The UNRRA was also directed to wind up its operations in Austria and be replaced by the IRO (International Refugee Organization). And by that time the numbers of the Admont camps residence dwindled down to a mere 500, with no more new transports arrived since spring of 1947. Others had moved on towards Germany using my overnight transports. I felt myself redundant with very little to do.

CHAPTER 11

A Lot of Love around the Corner.

The Love of my Life, Gertrude Stein

At this period of time, I was only 19 years old, and realized that I had no personal relations. I suddenly discovered how lonely I was in the world. No companions or social life and constantly on the road as a nomad. There was a young refugee girl called Gertrude Kager in the camp. She was petite and 20 years old, a good looking, educated girl. She was born in Slovenia and during the war she was forced into labour at an Austrian farm. Due to the treatment that she had received at that farm, she hated all Austrians. She was just as lonely as I was, and she decided that she would not return to Yugoslavia under a communist

Gertrude

regime. We became very good friends and I took her with me on some of my trips, and she enjoyed coming with me. Since the camp's moral rules stipulated that only married couples may share rooms, Trudy and I were married in August 1947.

Sixty of the Best Years of my Life

Finally I was happy, until her passing on the 29th January 2006. My world had been broken again I have never got over it or recovered and never will. I became a recluse and still am this present day.

We were married at the registry office at Admont. All Jewish couples that were married during my time in the camp had to follow the same procedure, as Jewish marriages were not legally recognised. We went on our honeymoon to the most picturesque lakeside location near Salzburg and stayed mostly with friends. Shortly after, the closure of the camp at Admont became imminent. Resident numbers diminished to a mere three hundred since no more transports were coming from the east.

The largest of our former residents were transferred into Germany to wait for immigration possibilities, and maintained in the meantime a good life by engaging in black market activities. This was not my lifestyle.

CHAPTER 12

Separation into Criminal Life.

Together with members of other Zionist groups, I made my way to Italy (and left Trudy behind in Admont), where serious activities and preparations took place to enlist and train recruits for the Israeli army, once the state would be proclaimed in October 1947. I was instructed to proceed to Italy forthwith and to resume my illegal activities. This direction was endorsed by the British who were in charge of me at Admont. This led to a bitter but short separation from my new wife. My role was to take refugees, whose numbers had built up, over the Italian alps by road to Israel. The Italians did not turn a blind eye to this occurrence. The trip was a long one. It took three days. On one of these journeys I was captured and imprisoned by the Italian authorities. I was eventually released with enormous aid and support from the British government. I have not told many people about this matter, as I promised to keep it confidential to save huge political embarrassment to the

British. I was released and forthwith I made arrangements for Trudy to rejoin me. She came over the Italian border in mid-winter, in deep snow, taking a ride in an Italian snow plough, over the Brenner Pass (I had arranged this).

After some great personal difficulties, we were finally reunited again in January 1948 in a camp in southern Italy (Naples) and have never let go of each other since then. We met a couple in that camp, George and Eva Affabauer. We became friends and they also immigrated to Brisbane and were very successful in the scrap metal business. Our life was more difficult in Italy than it was in Austria, since as refugees we had no freedom of movement within the country. Soon afterwards we joined a secret Jewish military training camp, run by the Jewish Brigade, who later merged with the Haganah, a Israel-based organisation formed in 1920 to fight the British mandate in Israel. They were also attached to the British Army – that is why there was so much secrecy. We trained in a remote orange plantation in the town of Bari, a port city. Training was tough with real weapons, and unarmed combat training. My little wife Trudy threw a large man around and around like a rag doll. Anyone who knew Trudy knew that she was capable of that. Small in size but big in heart and determination. You would not like to tangle with her. (My children and I know that very well).

Among 40 or so recruits I had 39 envious young men to contend with, especially in the mornings – when we did a three-kilometre run, she left us all behind! The only other woman in the camp was the commanding officer's wife, who was a professional nurse in charge of health and hygiene at the camp.

All instructors were former members of the Jewish Brigade, who had seen action at Monte-Casino. After a six-week course a festive graduation took place. A selected number of us who had passed the Hebrew language test graduated with honours and sent to a medieval castle near Turino for an advanced leadership and commando course. Trudy was restricted somewhat because the instructors would not let her take part in cross-country or night exercises. She told them what she thought of that. We finished our army training in Italy. Trudy attained the rank of sergeant. We then went on to do an officers course but did not complete it because the British wanted us out of Italy.

CHAPTER 13

Land of Milk and Honey 'Eretz Israel'

Finally the day arrived in early May 1948. A large luxury coach arrived at the castle. We were all given a large empty suitcase to give the impression that we were real passengers. We boarded the coach and were driven to the Rome Airport Military Section at midnight. We quietly boarded a waiting British Royal Airforce four-engine Lancaster bomber, piloted by South African Jewish volunteer pilots. We had blankets in the fuselage and the plane then took off for Haifa, Israel. My wife, the only woman on board, was offered the privilege of travelling on the flight deck where it was warm. She accepted on the condition that I could be with her. The boys in the fuselage nearly froze to death, as they were not provided with heavy warm clothing required for high altitude. At sunrise, we landed at the Ramat David Airbase near Haifa.

Heavy machine guns were unloaded from our plane on to the kibbutz 'Degania Alef', a co-operative society of mainly farms founded in 1910, where the profits are distributed to the residents (mainly volunteers) and run by the Jewish Agency. We left the airfield in normal civilian route buses, in small groups mixed with local passengers. This enabled us to pass the roadblocks of the British Army who still controlled the roads. We were deposited at the Haifa Technion (University of Technology) which served as an induction area for the army. We celebrated the Declaration of Independence for the State of Israel. There it was broadcast on radio from Tel Aviv.

The next day Trudy and I were inducted and sworn into the Israeli army and received our uniforms and our army numbers. It was a feeling of euphoria – we had made Aliyah at last – and also became citizens of Israel, a country for the first time in our lives that we were welcomed. I had fulfilled my pledge that I gave to the Zionist movement at Budapest in 1945. My wife was the first woman to be recruited and trained overseas. We became a part of the Haganah, the Zionist Jewish paramilitary group. It was formed by Ze'ev Jabotinsky with the express goal of defending the growing Jewish population in the British mandate of Palestine against the Arabs, and it was disbanded on the 28th May 1948. The group later became a part of the Jewish resistance against the British presence. It was the nucleus of the Israeli army.

Life was good in Israel. We settled in the suburb of

Bat Yam. My first son Reuben was born on the 27th February 1950, followed by Michael on the 20th January 1951. We both left full-time with the army and I became a reserve officer. I was lucky enough to get a position as a chauffeur for a well-known solicitor. He was a friend of my next-door neighbour and was trained in England. He was very generous and let me take the vehicle home on weekends. We travelled and explored by the Mediterranean Sea. We had lovely neighbours, the Yassamonki's, who were our best friends. We kept in contact with them and visited regularly from Australia. They were both young lawyers and now run one of Israel's top law firms, run by their daughters Rivka and Fenya.

'On the Move Again'

I felt that there was more for myself, Trudy and my two young children, so it was time for new beginnings. I finally decided the new opportunity would be in Australia. I heard so much about a free, open democratic country. I loved Israel – there was nothing against Israel – but the opportunities were not there. I fulfilled my dreams of many years about resettling, getting married and having children.

I loved the Zionist movement and Israel. Now two of my sons were born there and they also loved it there. I fought for the Israeli army for three years. The overriding factor for this move was for Trudy. Although she was not in a concentration camp, she lived in Yugoslavia with her parents and brother and sister, and then in Austria where during the war she was placed in a work camp at Admont. Her parents immigrated to Australia in 1949, so her parents were already here. I had my ambitions and goals to prosper in life and, as I stated earlier, at that time in Israel there were not many possibilities. I managed to scratch out an existence, but I was looking for some improvement because life is very short.

I was 20 years of age then and it was time to start a brand-new life. This offered us a golden opportunity which we took with open arms, so we came to Australia as unassisted immigrants.

We paid our own way without a contract with the Australian government. It was an open book. Thousands of immigrants, from mainly Italy, Greece and Europe, migrated and were welcomed. We came to Australia in 1956. In the meantime, before we arrived we had to wait two years in Israel for approval. At that time the White Australia policy was in place, and we had to be fully checked out.

My two children both had blonde hair. I also was blonde and Trudy had fair hair, so we looked very white and very Caucasian in appearance, so that represented no problem.

CHAPTER 14

Australia – The Lucky Country.

It was early January 1956 when we made our departure from Tel Aviv Airport. The day had finally arrived. We were all there: Trudy and my two sons, Reuben and Michael. They were both crying and shouting 'Ani Lo' in Hebrew ("I do not want to"). They were scared and had enjoyed their short lives in Israel, as we boarded the BOAC Super Constellation. The journey was a mammoth effort it took six days, with a multitude of stops. Now it takes 27 hours with one stop.

We finally arrived in Sydney on a sunny hot morning. We were full of elation and joy. I felt like kissing the ground of my new country. Our journey was not complete as yet, as Trudy's parents lived in Brisbane, which was going to be our permanent place of abode. We had to endure a 24-hour train journey from Sydney to Brisbane. On arrival we took a taxi to Trudy's parents' house at 26 Beatson Terrace, Grange, a suburb of Brisbane. In my excitement on arrival

I left my passport and all my papers in the taxicab. The honest taxi driver came back and returned them. I gave him my last two pounds. I was completely broke.

When we were greeted by Trudy's family she broke down and sobbed. After all the heartbreak and pain that she had suffered they were tears of joy. I was the happiest man alive.

A condition of our entry was that we had to have a place to stay. Trudy's parents came to Brisbane in 1949 from Admont, Austria, and before that lived in Maribor, Slovenia. We stayed with her father Joseph, his wife Caroline, son Paul and sister Lotte. It was not difficult for them to migrate as Trudy's father was a master jeweller, only one of only a handful who could engrave in gold. He opened a high-end manufacturing jewellery business with his son Paul. The business was called Kager & Kager. It was on the second floor of the city chambers building on the corner of Queen and Edward Streets in Brisbane. They were very successful and specialised in the manufacture of high-end jewellery with many wealthy clients. Their first apprentice was a fellow by the name of Wallace Bishop, founder of large retail jewellery chain, Wallace Bishop). By the way, Trudy was also a jeweller and did her apprenticeship before the war with her father.

I started walking the streets with my toolbox under my arm looking for work and to build my dream. I walked the streets for 48 hours and finally found a job in Fortitude Valley with a company called Jackson Transport. They were a trucking company that carried wool and other goods to the wharves. I worked for them as a mechanic. I walked from the Grange to Fortitude Valley every morning and afternoon a distance of 9.5 kilometres. Trudy made cold tea for me and put it into a wine carafe. My fellow workers thought that it was wine and that I was an alcoholic.

I worked on their fleet of trucks in their garage and, apparently, I was too diligent. I was doing the work of three men, lifting truck gearboxes on my own and finishing jobs within an hour and a half, which used to take them two days to do. My co-workers did not like that. The breaking point came when I repaired a forklift and tested it to see if the lifting equipment was working. I pulled the lever up to lift it and within a minute the foreman came over and said on the spot "You're fired! That's because you are not permitted to work the levers on the forklift as you do not have a forklift licence".

I had no idea about union demarcation. It was run by the wharf labourers. If they would have told me I would not have pulled lever. I worked there for a month, and I was left without a job again, just before Christmas. Many years later Mrs Jackson, the owners wife, became a regular customer of mine. She told me that she admired my work, my work ethic and past experiences. It was Christmas time. I was left jobless without any means of support for my family for that long. I went everywhere on the north side of Brisbane from Windsor and Lutwyche. I went from service station to service station. "Do you need anybody to work for you? I am a qualified motor mechanic."

I walked into a small service station on Bowen Bridge Road, next to the Brisbane General Hospital. The owners name was David Kemp. He was a godsend. I will never forget him. His mechanic was on holidays and he needed someone desperately. He put me on immediately we became personal friends – even when I was there for only six days. He lent me his car so that I could take my wife and children out for an outing, an example of true Australian kindness.

I had told Dave about my dream of opening my own car repair business. One day he told me that he knew about a service station run by a 75-year-old gentleman who had retired and wanted to get rid of it. It was then time for me to go out and to achieve my dream of starting my own successful car repair business. I had nothing to lose so I met him. He told me that all that he wanted was for me to buy the remaining petrol in his two petrol pumps.

This fellow's name was Roy Neuman, a stockily built six-foot three Aussie bushie. He also hauled timber from the pine forests at Kenilworth, west of the Sunshine Coast, some 80 kilometres from Brisbane. He also used to race Offenhauser speed cars at the Brisbane Exhibition Ground. He was a man of many talents and an incredible human being. Of course we became the best of friends. He was away a lot of times and my children used to look after his sick wife and run errands to the pharmacy and shops.

The garage was a small tin shed in the northern suburb

of Zillmere, 15 kilometres from central Brisbane. I was very unfinancial at that stage and anybody who immigrated from Israel – or any other country – was not entitled to any financial assistance from the Australian government. I contacted the Jewish Help in Need Society. They told me that they could be of assistance if I could provide a personal guarantee, but I decided that, as I did not know anyone here that could assist me, that I would approach Roy Neuman.

I explained the situation to him and he said that all he required was £100 for his stock of petrol and that he would give me the keys and walk away, and he was willing to carry me until I could repay him, interest free. We then shook hands and it happened. Roy Neuman was a saint. The only downside was that we could not lock it up at night, so I slept on the premises overnight. That was another godsend, as people would knock on the door at all hours of the night seeking repairs and I always obliged – and charged accordingly. That became a normal occurrence. I never said 'no' to anybody, as my family found out, and my dear wife was mother and father to my children. She never complained. It was the only mechanical repairer for miles.

Within two or three weeks I had enough to pay back Roy Neuman and to purchase new petrol stock. Before delivery I had to pay in cash. The same system remained with the Shell Company for years: no money, no petrol. The cars that I repaired were very old at that time, 1920s and 1930s models. I stayed at that tin shed for twelve months and established my credentials.

Zillmere was a very poor socio-economic area with most residents being ex-service returned servicemen, and immigrants living in government-assisted housing. There was a railway station, a large police station, newsagent, delicatessen, hardware shop, butcher, newsagency, state school and movie theatre. Zillmere grew to be a large industrial area with various factories. It became full of characters. Over the years the local newsagent Jim Thorley used to run the local SP betting shop on a Saturday afternoon with the local police sergeant Glen Sternberg being security and the bouncer. The early years in Zillmere were an eye opener.

CHAPTER 15

Shell Zillmere Driveway.

6th June 1956 – It was time to have a place of our own for our family and Trudy was pregnant. I had decided whilst I about to start my new venture. Roy Neuman owned a small two-and-a-half bedroom house with a lounge room, kitchen, outside toilet (in those days there was no septic or sewer connected), small bathroom and backyard (which was empty) at 390 Zillmere Road, Zillmere, Queensland. Next to his house, we rented. It was a five minute walk from my service station on the corner of Handford and Zillmere Road. We were finally settled in our own house. What an achievement! Four houses down was a small mixed business owned by Mr Levy, a Jewish survivor, so there was a bit of familiarity there with the past.

We needed transport so I bought an old beat-up Ford Customline. It did not look very appealing. I fixed it up and got it running. Trudy did her part also. I bought her a sewing machine and she refurbished the inside and the upholstery. We could now go on outings and visit Trudy's family at the Grange but, as expected, this very rarely occurred as I put in 24-and-a-half hour days, seven-and-a-half days a week. In establishing my business this worked out in the future, but I lost the opportunity of growing and communicating with my children which I came to regret for the rest of my life. Trudy was a hero, playing mother and father and bought me breakfast, lunch and dinner for over thirty years, and countless hours of pumping petrol, going for parts, cleaning the service station, and doing the banking. She never complained.

Renewing my Jewish Faith

I made a determination to bring up my family in a solid Jewish faith as my forefathers, and in respect to my departed parents. I contacted the rabbi of the Brisbane Synagogue, Dr Alfred Fabian, a very well-educated English man who made the effort to come to visit us at home with his young family. He was welcomed with open arms and a lifelong relationship with the Brisbane Jewish Community was established. He was very sympathetic with my past experiences and understood what I wanted to achieve in my family's work and personal life, and he enrolled my two sons into the *cheder*, a school where Jewish history and religion are taught. I volunteered to teach when possible on Sunday. He also arranged for pick-ups when I could not take them with Maurice Zavelsky and George Frey (who became my best friend). My children attended the first

Betar (Jewish youth group) camp at Alexandra Headland in 1956, and we all became connected with Betar for the next thirty or so years.

My son Frank became the Australian head of that movement, giving him the grounding for achieving greater things in life. Our involvement in Betar was to arrange the movement of food, goods and baggage to the camps and to help set the thing up. Trudy did all the shopping and cooking at the camps, with a loyal band of helpers including Bertha Zavelsky, Fay Frey, Pearl Sarragossi and Anna Cowen, the wife of Sir Zelman Cowan, the former Governor General of Australia, and many others. It was a labour of love for many years.

My involvement in the Brisbane Jewish community went further than that. I became involved with B'nai B'rith (Jewish Benevolent Society), State President of the Zionist Council, President of the South Brisbane Hebrew congregation.

The original synagogue at Deshon Street, Woolloongabba, was destroyed by a devastating fire in the early seventies. I went into action. I financed and purchased land on a vacant block on top of hill at Bunya Street, Greenslopes, and built a modern state-of-the-art synagogue on that land, including a five-metre menora which still adorns the front of the synagogue on top of that hill. I also bought a residence at the rear to accommodate a new rabbi that I had arranged to come from England. There was also a *mikvah* (Jewish ritual cleansing bath for females). I also arranged for the long-term loan of a Sefer Torah, a Jewish religious scroll containing the five books of Moses.

I was honoured at the 100th celebrations of the South Brisbane Hebrew congregation – a stained glass portrait of me. It hangs proudly in the synagogue.

Trudy was an integral cog in the building of the synagogue. She organised fund-raising functions, mainly bingo. It was a sight to see her going to these events in her red Suzuki Hatch with her beloved German Shepherd Mott sitting beside her in the front seat, with her helpers Ann Goldsmith and Dora Doobov cramped in the back. She also did all the sewing of the curtains, designing of the modern commercial kitchen, and did all of the catering.

I now attend the synagogue whenever I can, due to illness over the past few years and aided with the assistance of transport by the present president, Gary Goldman.

I was also the President of the Queensland Jewish Board of Deputies, and executive member of the Queensland Association of Jewish Ex-Servicemen & Women (QAJEX), and president of the Queensland Zionist Federation for many years. I was also the president of the Brisbane Chevra Kadisha (Jewish Burial Society) for many years.

My other great love, which I spoke about earlier in the book, is the Dora Memorial and Museum at Nordhausen in northern Germany. I first visited the Museum in 1990 after the unification of Germany from the Soviet Union. There I first met Professor Dr Jens Christen Wagner. He was the first director of the museum and is now in charge of all the museums in Germany. We have become very close friends over the years, and I assisted him with his thesis. I attend the memorial service on the 15th April each year.

My photo still stands proudly at the entrance of the museum. I have done an interview scripted by Dr Wagner of the award-winning documentary 'Dora – Concentration Camp of the "Total War"'. Also appearing in it is Simon Hersch Z"L from Sydney whose son David was the best friend of my son Frank. Also I am close to Professor Dr Karsten Uhl, who is the present director at Dora. I have also done documentaries for the British Broadcasting Federation about Bergen-Belsen ('The Living Hell') and German and Canadian Television.

I organized the first Holocaust Exhibition held in Brisbane at the Brisbane City Hall in 1982, under the patronage of Johannes Bjelke-Peterson and Sir Zelman Cowan (ex-Governor General of Australia). I was ably assisted by my friend George Frey who was a tailor, and he designed Holocaust striped pyjamas with a yellow star that I wore so many years ago at the death camps. I have also done radio television, and newspapers throughout Australia, teaching and spreading the story about the Holocaust. We have to remember. It did happen: six million Jewish people perished.

I have made a lifetime goal to teach and educate young people and others about the Holocaust. I have given lectures to many schools, community and other organizations. We must never, ever forget. Now as always antisemitism and discrimination abounds.

CHAPTER 16

Shell Zillmere Driveway, cont'd.

Changes were about to happen. The Shell Company wanted to build a state-of-the-art service station with a modern workshop and fuel bowser facilities. This is what I was dreaming about for years. I approached them and told them, "Look, I cannot offer you anything financially. The business was doing very well, but not as well as I anticipated, because Zillmere is not a wealthy suburb but is growing, with industrial sites and factories being built". I told them that all that I could offer is my diligence and my own hard work. I am in no position to purchase the first lot of fuel, or other required retail sales stock. To my surprise they accepted my offer – they must have done their homework.

Many years later I found out that were keeping their eye on me and had heard nothing but excellent reports about me. The Shell Company took a risk on me, which in those days was very rare. But I repaid the favour with

35 years as a loyal dealer. I had to take out an insurance policy and they agreed to give me a start-up loan, which was at that time A$3,000. That was to basically equip the retail shop and repair workshop, and this included the first load of fuel on a consignment basis. This was and still is unheard of, though I had to pay for the fuel as soon as it was sold. 'No credit account'.

So away we went. The opening was spectacular. We gave away lollies for the children, and other giveaways. We were swamped. There were eight petrol bowsers, four modern workshop bays. I installed an extension phone directly to home which never stopped ringing. I can still remember the telephone number, it was MY1691, and at last – finally – I could lock the door, and spend some time with my family (though this never happened). I was never busier and was fined several times for being open after hours. At that time the hours were regulated from 7 am to 6 pm Monday to Friday, and 7 am to 12 pm on Saturdays, and closed on Sundays. The state government Labour and Industry Department and my opposition wanted me closed, and not to operate after hours, but the public wanted me to remain open. I have never and will never say 'No' to anyone (except VW owners). It was a business to serve people and to make money to support my growing family.

I explained to the government inspectors, "Look, I am not doing any harm to anyone". Three kilometres down the road, on the Bruce Highway heading north, they had unrestricted opening hours and were open 24 hours a day. I explained to them that I am working for myself, by myself without employing or having anyone working for me after hours. I have debts to pay, a family to support, and customers are lining up for repairs at all hours. I was fined a few times but after that they let me off and left me alone. I got to know them and even helped them with repairs to their own cars after hours. I sold my old tin shed to a welding works.

Life did get easier at last. My first and only daughter was born. Our family was growing now, there were three children to support. My two sons Reuben and Michael were enrolled at Zillmere State School. No matter how poor we were then, Trudy made certain that they were dressed properly, wearing shoes and socks, and provided with morning tea and lunch, consisting of salami sandwiches made on fresh bread.

Zillmere was a very rough place in those days. It was survival of the fittest. Discrimination was rife. My children were bullied about their heritage relentlessly. For example, most of the children went to school barefoot. On one occasion, while walking home from school their shoes and socks were stolen and thrown into the creek beside the railway line. This came to an end swiftly. The headmaster and 90 per cent of the teaching staff became my regular customers.

Life was buzzing. There were a lot of things that I did differently from my opposition. I bought an ex-army surplus truck with a crane on the back, painted it in Shell colours and turned it into a tow truck. There were two hotels in the area, the Aspley Hotel and the Bald Hills Hotel. Both stood on steep hills. People used to have a few too many and selected the wrong gear and smashed over the retaining wall. The publicans both had my phone number with the extension phone at home and called me to recover the cars, as I was the only one with a tow truck in the area. It was a good money-earner for years.

I also became the first Royal Automobile Club of Queensland service agent, roadside assistance and author- ised repairer in the north Brisbane area. That lasted for many years. Another thing that I did was to put a kerosene tank on the back of the tow truck, and did a letterbox drop on Sundays in the area, and delivered heating kerosene to households for their heaters in winter. I also started giving 30-day credit accounts. This improved my customer base, and company accounts with new factories and industrial buildings being established in the area, and my cash flow immensely.

Momentum was expanding at a huge rate in the business. I had two bowser attendants, two full-time mechanics and I employed my first apprentice mechanic. I obtained a large contract which lasted for over 25 years with a company called Nutta Products/Daffodil Peanuts and MeadowLea margarine. I serviced and repaired their fleet of trucks and cars overnight and on weekends. This was followed by contracts with companies like ASEA, Olympic Rubber and General Products, and various other companies. This was helped along by me becoming a foundation member of the Rotary Club of Geebung. I was honoured by the club with becoming an inducted Paul Harris Fellow, the highest award in the Rotary movement.

What made life interesting at the service station was the characters that were attracted from all different walks of life. There was a large group of Italians in the area. One of these was Charlie Nardo who had a large vegetable farm on Handford Road, which he sold many years later for a fortune to developers who built retirement villages and town houses, and he had a fruit shop in the shopping strip. We were supplied by him for many years with the best fruit and vegetables.

Roy Newman always came to have a chat and visit when he was around. One day he bought his mate along: Archie Shoemaker, also a large bushie who always wore a battered Akubra hat and never without a roll-your-own cigarette hanging out of his mouth. His position was sitting on an empty kerosine drum by the front door. He stayed from lunchtime and left just before 3 pm sharp, as he could not stand the noise that the school children made walking home from school.

Another fellow by the name of Kev O'Gorman was a railway worker with twelve children. As he was doing it tough, I helped him out many times with petrol. People thought that I was a rich, mean wog bugger, but if they only knew about my past. I have never sought praise or boasted about helping others. It makes me feel good. His children turned out alright and were very successful. I met many of them years later and they always gave me a hug. One of his sons, John O'Gorman became a high ranking police officer and then the president of the Police Union. His son Terry is a well-known criminal defence solicitor and runs a very large law firm; his other son Dan O'Gorman is a barrister and Queens Council; and his daughter Kate O'Gorman is Queens Council.

We had high ranking politicians that lived in Zillmere, mainly Frank Sleeman, an ex-World War two veteran who was incarcerated by the Japanese and worked on the famous Burma Railway. He became Lord Mayor of Brisbane. He was a straight-shooter who did not mince his words. He lived on Zillmere Road in a small well-kept house next to O'Callaghan Park, the home of Windsor-Zillmere Australian Rules Football Club.

There was a young boy who used to ride his bike between cars and the bowsers at breakneck speed. I used to chase him around the driveway endlessly with a long-handled broom and yell out obscenities in a loud voice that woke the dead. Anyone that knows me can testify what it is like when I get annoyed. I never caught him. He was too fast. I found out from my son Benny that it was none other than Mick Doohan, five-time Grand Prix F1 Motorcycle world champion. He also had lived in Zillmere and went to school with Benny at Aspley High School.

There were more tales to tell. One fellow came in one

day and in an old utility with sheep in the back. He could not pay for his fuel, so he left a goat for me. I took it home and the children tied it up around the neck with a rope, and they played in the backyard with it. But all good things must come to an end. The council found out about the goat. It was illegal to keep goats on residential properties and they came and removed it. It broke my children's heart.

On the 5th December 1958 my third son Frank Daniel Stein was born. It was a very difficult birth. He was born premature and a blue baby, and only weighed six pounds, if I remember rightly. We nearly lost him a couple of times, but miracles happen and he survived. He grew up large in heart, compassion and stature, but that did not last. It is a very sad story that shook us all to the core. There is more to come later in this story.

My fifth and youngest son was born on the 5th March 1960. Finally, Trudy's and my dreams were accomplished. We were a complete family life was now perfect.

CHAPTER 17

Our Final Home:
28 Fernlea Street, Geebung.

We were still living in our small house at Zillmere with five children. We brought the house for cash with the hard work that we put in. There were a couple of major incidents that had occurred and made rethink and reevaluate our circumstances, going forward and looking towards the future. We had an old kerosene heater to keep the family warm in winter. One night whilst I was working, as normal, it caught fire. Trudy raced across the road to Robert Young's house and sought his assistance. He was a retired British Army Sergeant-Major and a lovely man. He rushed over to our house with a blanket and immediately took the burning heater out to the backyard and extinguished the fire by covering the heater with the blanket making sure it was extinguished properly.

On another occasion, on a Saturday afternoon, a drunk

driver was driving along Zillmere Road and lost control of his vehicle, and he went through Roy Neuman's front fence. Luckily he did not hit any of Roy's old trucks, trailers or assorted machinery scatted throughout his yard. It went through our side fence and came to a sudden halt. Also as luck would have it, he just missed hitting the side of our house where our young children were watching television. My tow truck came in handy again to remove the car, and you should have seen the look on his face when he was confronted by all six-foot-one of angry me, in my loud boisterous voice yelling classic Australian bush profanities at him. This was followed immediately by old mate Sergeant Glen Sternberg, the local police sergeant, who was also six-foot-tall, arriving and giving the stunned, fearful car driver some good old-fashioned justice.

Business was booming at the service station especially on a Saturday morning. We traded from 7 am until midday. Trudy worked the petrol bowsers with my brother-in-law Paul. It was a full-service site, petrol, oil, water and tyres were checked and all windscreens cleaned.

The routine would be: the customer would arrive; he was greeted with a welcoming "Hello, how are you?"; fuel sold; everything checked, always with no short cuts taken. "Mr or Mrs Customer, you need oil, your tires need replacement, you have a faulty battery, your wiper blades are worn out". 99 per cent of the time they bought something or had repairs done to their cars, and as an extra benefit they were given thirty days credit. We had no real problem with the customers paying their bills. For those who did not or were behind, they used to get a friendly knock on their door at lunch time Sunday – that is when they are always home having lunch with their family. I knocked on the door in company with Reuben and Michael with their sad eyes looking at the person. This always worked, and we got paid on the spot, and with the guilt and the embarrassment that they felt this never happened with them again. Human psychology at work. If it ever did, I knew they would come in one day or night and want something urgently done and I would gladly tell them to go away in my loud boisterous voice and expressions. Also, on Saturday mornings, my sons Reuben and Michael would arrive early and clean the site, refill the empty oil bottles and check the customers oil, tyres and battery, and clean the windscreens. They learnt early in life.

We were supposed to lock the bowsers at midday, but we did not. My sons were still there serving petrol. Later on we had a 24-hour coin pump installed, the first one on the north side of Brisbane. We left them on manual until 6 pm on Saturdays because there were people everywhere wanting petrol. Reuben and Michael stayed there also, because a lot of people did not have any change, so it was easier and a lot more profitable to fill their cars up or give them what they required. Meanwhile I was flat out in the workshop working on company vehicles and mainly trucks. The coin pumps turned out to be cash cows. The only downside is that Trudy or I had to go and empty the cash boxes regularly as they were always full. Trudy stayed up and counted and sorted the coins and banked them. We had a special counter and person allocated at the bank to bank the coins. The staff at the bank could not believe the amount that we deposited.

I built up a good relationship with the manager at the National Bank Linday Ellwood, and with John Fairbairn, who later became Queensland State Manager. I had his direct line phone number, and he told me to ring him any time for any reason (I never did that). He invited me to lunch at the bank's Brisbane head office.

Business was so good that I bought a brand-new car, a Ford Falcon Classic station wagon. TV had commenced and I bought a new black-and-white one for my family. Occasionally as a family we would go on picnics and drives, but again this time it was not work at the garage, but Sunday mornings were devoted to doing paperwork and bills. Trudy would not let me do the monthly statements for customers or the banking. She sat there in the kitchen in the corner by herself on a typewriter and work away endlessly for hours.

The children also had a small canvas pool in the back yard. I still have a photo of them in it which is one of my prized possessions.

Finally, the move
We decided finally to upgrade our premises. With seven

children, and the experiences with the fire, and the car smashing into our house, we built ourselves a brand new five-bedroom double-storey brick house on top of a hill at 28 Fernlea Street, Geebung, in a new estate where six Mater Prize Homes were built. It was only four kilometres from the service station. It ended up our forever home, for over 65 years. We all used to go and inspect it at nighttime, and on the first inspection we sat on the bare newly-poured concrete slab, hugged each other and cried forever (I do not know how long) with tears of exhilaration and heartfelt joy.

'We had finally arrived'
I rented out our old house, and then sold it twelve months later for a healthy profit. There are townhouses on the land now, but Roy Neuman's huge house and land are still there. I wonder if his pride and joy, his Offenhauser speed car is still stored in the garage. We paid cash for our dream house £6,000 ($10,000). The house has three bedrooms upstairs with two bedrooms downstairs, and toilet and shower upstairs, and a second toilet and shower downstairs, with a two-car garage and large workshop area where I can potter around to my heart's content with a lathe, large work bench with power outlets, large upright industrial drill shelves, and a multitude of tools and gadgets that I have collected over the years. A real man shed.

We used to sit on the front terrazzo balcony having coffee on Sunday afternoon as a happy family and watch as a multitude of cars drove past looking at the prize homes. We sat there and waved at them.

Trudy loved gardening. She planted trees and garden beds, and filled them with a multitude of various plants. Both the front and backyards were showpieces. No one was allowed to mow or touch the lawn except her. It was immaculate. What else would you expect from her? I taught her how to drive and bought her a three-cylinder blue Fiat Bambi with a sunroof. But as you can appreciate, it was unreliable. It looked good, but I always had to tow it back for repairs and fix it. It was the laughing joke of the suburb. She finally got her own way and I bought her a more reliable car, a brand new Hillman IMP.

I was at work at 6 am each day, and Trudy would bring down morning tea and lunch every day for over thirty years but, as always, she never ever complained. Also the countless nights she dropped me off or picked me up in the middle of the night or early in the morning to collect or return repaired trucks.

Charlie Nardo used to deliver fresh fruit and vegetables to our house once a week, along with Norbert Sturm, a German who along with his wife Elsa had a delicatessen next to the Zillmere Railway Station. She brought groceries and continental smallgoods to us every week. We had it all organized. I never forgave the German people or forgot, but in later years I have become a lot more tolerant with the friends that I have made, including Richard and Eva Vogel. Richard was an artist and painted a magnificent painting for her that is still hanging in our lounge room. Eva became Trudy's best friend. My mother-in-law, Caroline Kager, moved in with us and lived in one of the downstairs bedrooms after her husband, Trudy's father, Joseph Kager, died, and she stayed with us for five years until her death.

I suppose that you could call us extravagant. I had a master cabinet-maker make a large customised wall unit covering the whole wall including, bookshelf, glass display cabinets, radio, record player and storage shelves, made out of teak. It still stands as new in perfect condition till now. Trudy had an elderly German lady, Mrs Herman, come over and make curtains and clothing for her and the children.

CHAPTER 18

My Children are Growing Up.

Life is hectic but that is normal in the Stein world. My children attended Zillmere State School and Aspley State High School. My eldest son Reuben was one of the first enrolments when the high school first opened in 1963. They made lots of friends and were all very popular. Then jealously raised its ugly head, "Your father is the rich Jew that owns the service station". But my children had the strength and fortitude to overcome this obstacle and antisemitism.

My business was expanding. The site had a refurbishment to bring it in line with current trends. Two extra service bays were added, 24-hour coin-operated carwash, completely new fuel bowsers – "the old ones were worn out from use" – an expanded retail and merchandising area (Shell Shop). And I had three full-time driveway attendants with improved full service.

With two full-time apprentices, Robert and Mark, who

remained loyal and served me wholeheartedly for many years. Robert confided in me many years later that when he first started as a 15-year-old boy he was terrified of me, but that soon changed. I treated them both as if they were my children, so did Trudy. She gave them both a big hug when she saw them. After my retirement they both joined forces together and opened their own vehicle repair business at the suburb of Deagon. I used to go and visit them and ended up being there for hours, but as always Trudy did not complain. They were flat out and gained a solid reputation. Of course they succeeded because I taught them both the right work ethic.

I had a friend who had a small car repair workshop at Chermside called Timms Autos. He wanted to establish a new Ford dealership in the area but was short of the funds required, and wanted a silent partner to help him financially. I agreed and the dealership was established. It became Timms Ford, then sold later for a tidy profit to Bert and Betty Byrne and is now known as Byrne Ford.

I continued with my long hours of work. My mantra then and still is: you do not have to like someone to take their money.

I remember one time, it was very early in the morning and I was under a truck. All of a sudden an expensive sports car pulls up in front of the workshop, and screeched to a halt and blew his horn. He yelled out, "My bloody car is playing up! Will you fix it?". I had a look and made the necessary adjustment to the carburettor and, as always, charged him accordingly. He then shouted out, "You screwed me". I replied, "Yes I did, but I knew what screw to turn."

My other thing that I will always believe is, and learnt a long time ago: "Without customers you do not have a business". These days the art of customer service and listening have completely disappeared.

As always, I continued working my long hours, along with Rotary and many varied Jewish communal activities which I enjoyed and came very involved with. My two sons had piano lessons with Sister Roberta at St Flannan's Catholic Parish School. We also bought them a piano so that they could practise. Many years later I taught myself to play, but not very well and the family used to run away and hide on hearing my attempts.

What many people do not know is that Trudy's family were very strict Catholics. She was studying to be a novice nun when the war broke out. The first request that she put to Rabbi Fabian so many years ago was that she wanted to be recognised as being Jewish. He granted this request immediately. Also on rare specials occasions she snuck away and attended Catholic mass. She thought that I would not find out but I did, as I had my spies everywhere and never told her. Of course I did not mind.

All of my children always regularly attended Betar camps in August each year, along with Trudy and her merry band of helpers. They also attended leadership camps in Sydney each December. They studied and completed their bar mitzvahs at the age of 13, also Hannah who had her bat mitzvah.

My eldest son Reuben has a very high IQ, and my dream was for him to become a doctor. Maybe I pushed him too hard, a normal Jewish European trait. He started studying medicine for a few years, but he changed direction mid-stream, and went to the bigger and brighter lights of Melbourne with some friends. He did end up being a male matron in later life, specialising in aged care and mental health.

In December 1966 my second son Michael, who is the spitting image of me in temperament, and very strong willed and adventurous, decided to join the Royal Australian Navy for twelve years, at the age of 16 and a half. He joined as a junior recruit and went to HMAS *Leeuwin*, training school at Fremantle in Western Australia, to do one year's study to achieve his high school matriculation. He told me many years later that because he was Jewish and the local rabbi came and visited him, and he was given special leave to attend the Perth Synagogue on Saturday mornings with transport provided, that he was subject to antisemitism, intimidation, serious assault and bullying by the senior recruits and training instructors. Many years later an inquiry was set up chaired by a High Court Judge Rapke (who was Jewish). The Rapke Report found that the allegations were true and condemned these actions. But his strong will like mine overcame this hurdle in life. I was shocked when told of this and I asked him, "Why did you not tell me about this earlier? I would have sorted it out straight away for you". He told me not to worry about it. It was in the past and life must go on. I was and still am very proud of him.

Trudy attended his graduation in Fremantle in December 1967. He saw active service for twelve years including active service in Vietnam and attained the rank of Petty Officer Coxswain in the Regulating Branch. He retired from the services due to horrific circumstances, when his daughter Rachel Michelle, our first grandchild, passed at the age of six months and two days old of Sudden Infants Death Syndrome, SIDS, when a baby falls into a deep sleep and ceases to breathe.

To say that 28 Fernlea Street was the hub of activity was an understatement and realistic. All of my children's friends used to call by and visit. It occurred regularly. We billeted athletes competing at the Maccabi Games. Interstate youth came and stayed often. I even hosted a reception for the visit to Brisbane of the Israeli Philharmonic Orchestra, conducted by Zubin Mehta.

It was a friendly open-door policy always at our house. Everyone was welcome. Trudy sitting in the same chair with her trusty Alsatian Mott cuddled by her side, smoking Camel or Capstan plains with no filter (at least eighty a day). I was not allowed to complain, and had to order and buy them from my wholesalers, Tickles, whilst she was knitting and drinking copious amount of strong black coffee, and also listening or watching the cricket on the

ABC on the small tv that I had to mount on a bracket on the wall above her. All of this was done simultaneously, whilst being the conductor and leader of the boisterous, discussions and conversations, and with words of wisdom and advice for support for the problems of the world. This occurrence happened thousands of times.

To have Friday night (Shabbat) dinner with the whole family, was compulsory to attend, or face the wrath of Trudy. The white linen scalloped tablecloth would be laid on the unreplacable ten-seater extendable teak dining room table, gifted to the family from Trudy's mother, the irreplaceable Rodd stainless steel cutlery, and Wedgewood dinner sets. There were different patterns to choose from. Trudy would painstakingly bake two loaves to perfection, and when we all arrived the gastronomic feast would start. Firstly I was always admonished by Trudy for not cutting the challah properly by chopping the bread, not sawing it. I would never learn and I was useless – she always screeched at me. There was an endless list of guests that partook in that ritual. There was always an extended wait list. As expected the feast was spectacular as can be verified by all that did attend.

In the early years Michael and Reuben, who had left the roost, were missing in action but returned later in time with their meshuggener throng. This event was to be seen to be believed with lively debate, discussions and everything else, the same as before just transferred from the kitchen to the dining room. The only thing different was that I was present. After the four course degustation we would all retire to the lounge room for coffee and cake and the festivities would continue.

Hannah Stein

My only daughter Hannah remained living with us for a few years, she studied Sports Psychology and Early Childcare, and became very involved in Rotaract (Rotary Young Adults Group).

Benny Stein

Our youngest son Benny was very artistic and started doing ballet lessons at the age of six, with private lessons at home. He was taught by Barbara Everson and later danced with the Queensland Youth Ballet with a young girl by the name of Karen Hoskins. Karen became Michael's second wife many years later. Benny also developed itchy feet and decided to spread his wings and immigrated to Israel on Mahon Youth Learning experience at a kibbutz called Kiryat Moriah in Jerusalem, which is now the Jewish Agency Headquarters, where my third son Frank had his office later as the Australian representative of the Zionist Federation.

On returning to Australia in 1978 he made Aliyah to Israel and studied the arts, later teaching at the University of Tel Aviv. He did two years compulsory army service also in Tel Aviv, which is required for all Israelis between the ages of 18 and 20. In 1994 Benny married his wife

Yael here in Brisbane. I paid for their wedding and bought them both out. They have two children Noa and Tair, one is studying to be a doctor and the other is in university studying psychology. I travel to see them all every two years and they have visited us twice. I bought them a house in Tel Aviv as a wedding present.

Frank Daniel Stein, more pain

My third son Frank was a miracle after his premature birth and many complications. He was larger than life and the perfect child that every parent would want. He was very popular at school and became very involved in the Betar youth movement, like the rest of my children. He rose to become Australian head of Betar, and then promoted to the position of Australian head of Hannai youth movement at the Central Synagogue in Bondi, Sydney, under the mentorship of Rabbi Aloni. His main task at the synagogue on Shabbat was to sit in between Frank Lowy and Harry Triguboff and keep order and decorum as they had heated discussions which kept on interrupting the service. Of course they got to know Frank very well and respected him for the rest of his life. Frank made Mahon to Jerusalem in 1982 and became the Australian Director Israel at Kiryat Moriah, head office of the Jewish Agency which I was a part of many years ago. I also bought him a flat in Jerusalem. I was very happy that two of my children who were born in Australia continued their Jewish heritage. They did me proud like all of them.

Frank was known by thousands of people from around the world, including the Israeli president and prime ministers. His main function was to welcome and assist young people on 'Aliyah' (resettlement, Mahon, or gap year), not only from Australia but from all over the world on their arrival in Israel. He also represented the British and American Olim Associations. He even had an unrestricted full security pass at Tel Aviv Airport.

When Trudy and I went to visit, which was yearly, we would be met at the aircraft door with hugs, tears and the largest smile on his ever-radiant face. We also could not hide our emotions. To give you all an idea of his generosity and compassion, someone told me that there was a young girl who arrived and was not very financial. Frank went guarantor for her accommodation and paid for it and also provided living expenses and furniture. What a *mensch* (Yiddish meaning: a person of the highest integrity and honour, a very kind person). He travelled all over the world and would visit with us once a year so that he could go to the Brisbane Exhibition.

On the 14th July 1999, whilst the World Maccabi Games were held in Tel Aviv, Israel, the bridge crossing the Yarkon River collapsed whilst athletes were crossing it. Two Australian participants were killed and sixty were injured. Frank rallied his team to give aid and comfort and to communicate with their relatives back home in Australia.

While on assignment in Johannesburg, Frank collapsed.

He was taken to hospital and diagnosed with appendicitis. They were removed immediately and he recovered. Later on, while on assignment again in London for the British Olim Association, he collapsed again and took another turn which he recovered from.

Frank heard that there was an opening for a Youth Leader Shelagh at the Zionist Federation of Australia. He applied and was told by the executive board to come to Melbourne for a quick meeting with them at the annual general meeting and conference, and they would have a discussion about it with him. He was in seventh heaven. He wanted to come home so badly, as he had been in Israel for 24 years and was homesick. His only wish was that he wanted to see Australia, his birth country and finally get time to be able to reconnect with his family, nephews and niece. He was over the moon with excitement and full of joy. He paid for the airfare and accommodation out his own pocket. At the conference he asked about the interview and was told that there would be no interview, and that they gave the position to someone else, and to go back to Jerusalem immediately and get back to work.

He resigned immediately on the spot, and they were shocked and tried to sweettalk him, but Frank did not care or say a word and walked out. He was devastated and heartbroken. He flew straight home and told me. I was also devastated and the angriest that I had ever been for years. Ever since that day I have never and will never have anything to do with the Zionist Federation of Australia, after being a loyal Zionist for over eighty years. The hierarchy changed, and politics took over. That the last time any of our family, except for Benny, ever saw our beloved Frank.

CHAPTER 19

The Tears are Still Flowing.

Frank went back to Jerusalem after he sent some quality time with the family and his friends, and was welcomed with open arms by the Jewish Agency and the Olim Society. His reputation with them was rock solid and a hero. I was told that he was in a strange place by many of his friends and became a hermit.

He lost all interest and was wandering the streets of Jerusalem without purpose or direction aimlessly. But he had a multitude of people that watched out for him, mainly David Hersh. They were best friends since Hennai and Betar days, and both had immigrated at the same time. David's father Simon Hersh, now deceased, was in forced-labour with me at Dora, and also appeared on Prof Wagner's *Dora* DVD).

Frank became very sick and contacted Peter Singer, Franks other best friend (his father Morrie Singer was among the British Forces that liberated me from the hell hole at Bergen-Belsen). He flew from Melbourne to Israel immediately with his wife, who is Israeli, to be at his bedside. They cooked, looked after his many cats, did his washing and comforted him. No one could wish for better friends.

Frank's condition deteriorated and was diagnosed with stage four bowel and kidney cancer. He was admitted to the Hadassah Ein Kerem Hospital and given chemotherapy treatment, which caused a fatal reaction. Frank passed on the 30th March 2009, aged 51, three years after I lost my dear beloved wife Trudy. My daughter Hannah rushed to be at his bedside but she did not arrive in time. It was too much grief and pain for me to go after his passing. We sat 'Shiva' (a week long mourning period for departed Jewish people) and recited 'Kiddush'. I went to visit his grave three months later with my son Benny and his family, with his long-time friend David Hersh, who lives in Israel, and other close friends of Frank's. Both Reuben and Michael went to visit his grave. We recited Kiddush. It was a solemn occasion.

A memorial plaque stands proudly on the door of his office at the Jewish Agency, with his name still on the door with the instructions never to be removed. There is also a memorial pergola which has been erected in the garden area where Frank used to sit and chew the fat with young people from all over the world. It bears a plaque with the names of those who donated funds to erect it, including Frank Lowy, John Saunders, Harry Triguboff, Isi Leibler, and many others.

I thought that after liberation, so many years ago, it would end, but not so. There is still more to come.

When Will It End?

I was told that the day of Frank's funeral was a perfect sunny day. It was held in Jerusalem. Frank lies at rest in peace on top of the hill overlooking his beloved city of Jerusalem where he belongs in the cemetery. The funeral service was very large, with over seven hundred people attending, including high profile politicians such as the Australian ambassador James Larsen who was a very close friend to Frank. No surprise that Frank and he were very close friends, they used to sit together in the air raid shelter when the air attacks occurred.

The news of Frank's death was broadcast worldwide and even made the Turkish newspapers. Years earlier an Australian Federal politician went to Israel on a trade mission, and I was told by him that he was greeted by Frank at the airport in a Brisbane Broncos Rugby League jersey. There is still a dedicated page to Frank on Facebook 'In memory of Frank Stein Z"L.'

CHAPTER 20

Life Goes On.

Now that most of the children have gone their own ways to find out and discover what life is all about. Hannah is the only one living with us at home. Life is a little bit less hectic now. The service station has had another major re-build in 1971 to modernise it. I now have very dependable, trustworthy staff, Robert and Mark, who are now top-notch qualified mechanics. Now we can travel and go to see our children, grandchildren and friends in Israel. We visited other countries to meet up with old friends. I took Trudy on a luxury cruise on the *Queen Elizabeth II* from Southampton across the Atlantic to New York. It was her dream experience.

In 1973 my second son Michael married a non-Jewish girl. We are not happy, but what can we do? We attended the wedding in Sydney. They seem to be happy. They had a daughter, Rachel, in February 1977. At last we have grandchildren. We went and visited them. Then disaster struck it's ugly head again. Their daughter was put down to have a sleep one afternoon. He went to wake her but there was no movement. She was dead. She had died of SIDS (Sudden Infants Death Syndrome). It is caused when a baby goes into a deep sleep and they stop breathing. There still is no cure for this horrid occurrence. It shattered him and he has never got over it. I understand because of the traumas that I have had in the past.

We went to the funeral. It was a very sad occasion. Michael told me that he wanted to get away from it all and start a new direction in life. I suggested that he comes home to Brisbane and help me manage the business, and take over one day as I was not getting any younger and also getting tired. He did this in December 1978. He resigned from the Navy and moved to Brisbane with his wife. They bought a house at Bracken Ridge and joined me in running the business. It will be ongoing.

I was very pleased. They had another daughter, Rebecca. Trudy and I were over the moon. I was a gloating grandfather. One Sunday afternoon, he came home after a Lions Club conference and found his house had been emptied out of everything and deserted. His wife had taken it all, including his daughter, and moved back to Blacktown to her parents. Things became very difficult between both of us and we started arguing, as we are very similar and very headstrong. Trudy stepped in and took control, as always, and said that things would not work out, and the best thing was for Michael to move on. He did this and even though he is my son and love him as much as all of my children, I could not forgive him and never will for doing this. I always remember and never forget or forgive. We did mend the bridges somewhat later in life, but the sadness, sorrow and pain will always be there.

Life was still very hectic. I was re-building the new synagogue at Greenslopes after the fire. It had been opened with a new Rabbi in place. Trudy was an enormous help in organising a multitude of successful fund-raising events. She was a great supporter of the National Council of Jewish Women and was the state president. She was also known for the annual Melbourne Cup luncheon held at home each November. I was banned from attending by her. I was very busy anyway with my other long-term activities, including president of the South Brisbane Jewish Congregation, president of the Chevra Kadisha, and president of the Zionist Federation. Seeing that I wanted to relive the youth that I never had earlier because of previous experiences, I indulged and bought a minibike. They were in fashion. It was a sight: six foot one me with a large frame covered by a helmet and goggles riding it to the service station. But all good things must come to an end and it was commandeered by the children who had many heated arguments on whose turn it was to ride it up and down the street and the main road. Luckily they all survived but, as always, all hell broke loose when I sold it (for a healthy profit).

I won a prestigious Distinguished Dealer Award whilst

attending a Shell Company conference at Bribie Island, a holiday island 45 kilometres north of Brisbane. The only way to get there in the late 50s was by car ferry. The waiting queues were very long and a bridge was built linking the island to the main land in the early 60s. I saw this beautiful corner block of land that was for sale on the corner of Broom and Lowry Street with a For Sale sign on it not far from the surf beach. I bought it straight away and did not tell Trudy as it was going to be a surprise for all of her years of loyalty and love to us all. I finally took Trudy on a secret drive and showed her the land. Once again we were in tears.

I arranged for one of my customers Bill Meuleman, a top notch builder (of German descent but a nice fellow) to design and build a three-bedroom low-set brick house on the block. I do not know how, but I spent hours laying carpet and tiles, establishing lawns and a small garden bed. It was a true labour of love. Trudy did not want to spend hours cutting the grass and playing in the garden because there was always a heatwave and she was there to relax. As long as she had her coffee, knitting, cricket, an endless supply of smokes, and Mott at her feet, she was always content.

As always there was a pecking order and the usual debates amongst or children as to who and when they were going. They wanted to go on their own without other brothers or sisters hanging around. We all enjoyed Bribie for years. I bought a four-wheel drive to explore the ten miles of unpopulated beaches and fishing.

Bert Payne, who had a grocery shop next to the garage, also had a house there, so Trudy and I spent time with them. We loved our little hideaway at Bribie and intended to spend our later years there in harmony. Many years later, due to work and communal activities and the children with other activities, no one went there often. Also the neighbour across the road, a just-retired TAA senior pilot who had a huge double-story house, went on a cruise with his wife, and while on that cruise he jumped over the side of the cruise ship. That scared me, and I received an offer that I could not refuse, so I sold it. Trudy never forgave me for selling it, maybe because I did not tell her. I was too scared.

CHAPTER 21

Wedding Bells. More Grandchildren.

Our only daughter Hannah was married on the 4th July 1984 to a young solicitor. They were married in a civil ceremony at Lennons Hotel in Brisbane. I contacted an uncle of mine living in France who came with his son and stayed with us. It was pleasant to spend time with them. Hannah's husband Chris was very successful and became a senior executive with Suncorp Bank. They did not have any children. Over the years I have assisted them in purchasing several houses. But due to circumstances they have divorced and Hannah now lives by herself.

In July 1986 my second son Michael met a girl, Karen Hoskins. It's a small world, as Karen and Benny performed together along with Barbara Everson at Ballet Theatre Queensland together. She did her schooling in Brisbane and was accepted into the Victorian College of the Arts. It was a very selective process. On graduating became a member of the Queensland Ballet, where she is now a member of the Alumni. She moved to England for three years to continue dance studies at Princess Dance Centre Covent Gardens, as well as working to support herself, then came back home to Brisbane and started teaching as a qualified ARAD examiner. They are very happy; she is a very nice girl. Trudy gets on very well with her and Trudy says it is the best thing that ever happened to Michael and that she is the only one that can control him and keep him in line (just like me).

Reuben, my eldest, worked in Cairns and Brisbane as a male matron, and in June 1986 married a local girl who was studying to be a lawyer. They had two children, Nick and Joseph (who is named after Trudy's father Joseph Kager). Things also did not go as they had expected for them and they separated. Reuben has lived downstairs in our house for the last twenty years or so. We both had Nicky and Joey on weekends and holidays. We nurtured them how to be good grandchildren and citizens – and spoiled them rotten of course. My favourite part was taking them to McDonalds and Trudy took them down to the local children's playground and bike track at Marchant Park. Trudy taught Nick the love of cricket. She used to take him to the matches and cricket tests at Woolloongabba with our neighbour Dulcie Townsend, who was a member of the Brisbane Cricketer's Club. He is now heavily involved at the Toombul Cricket Club.

I remember when many years later Nick came to Trudy and told her that he wanted to go to schoolies (a celebration with parties for high school graduates) at the Gold Coast with his friends, and he asked if he could have an advance on his birthday present. She replied saying there are conditions: do not get drunk and get locked up; do not get any young girls pregnant; or sneak alcohol in to apartment; keep the apartment tidy; and clean the oven. He agreed "Yes, I will do that Grandma", and was rewarded very handsomely and of course he behaved admirably.

Nick wanted to make a career in the hospitality industry. His mother Anne's family owned the Normanby Hotel, a popular hotel in Brisbane on weekends, frequented by young people. Nick started out doing his apprenticeship by picking up glasses, and worked his way up to being senior venue manager the with Woolworths ALH Hotel group. He is very much liked with a large circle of friends. He is the spitting image of my late son Frank, a very kind-hearted, smiling gentle giant in all aspects.

Joey on the other hand is the complete opposite, like his father and Trudy. He is very quiet and reserved and very intelligent. He has his own accountancy business on the Sunshine Coast, Stein Accounting, which is very successful with glowing reviews.

CHAPTER 22

The End Of an Era. Goodbye Shell Zillmere Driveway. The Retired Life.

1984 – time for a cool change (like the song from The Little River Band). I had put in over 35 years of blood sweat and tears into Shell Zillmere. I had many good times and many long and winding roads, but I conquered them all, and made a very good living and supported my family well.

I had terrific support from the Shell Company in the early days which I will never forget, and they received loyal support from me. Times were changing quickly. The company took on a new face with self-service, no driveway service, and they would rather sell cigarettes, lollies and groceries instead of repairing cars. It was all profit in their own greedy pockets, with greedy, self-serving bureaucrats who never knew you and never wanted to know you, and were uncontactable. What had happened?

Zillmere also changed as a suburb, with the industrial area being sold for the development of units, townhouses and retirement villages. The local shopping strip had become a ghost town. People were going to large multi-function shopping centres with cinemas, etc. The final straw for me was when one night, when I was locking up at about 9 pm. I was robbed and severely assaulted. That was the end for me, I gave up. Maybe it was a good sign from above. It even made the Channel 9News.

I put the site up for sale. Finally Trudy could have me for herself. After so many years she was happy. I could sell the lot, as I bought the land many years ago and paid for all the refurbishments myself. The Shell Company regarded me as an independent and had no say. It was snapped up in no time, for a healthy profit of course. To my surprise, Shell rewarded Trudy and me with a celebration dinner and presented me with a prestigious award for being the longest-serving dealer in Queensland. The new owner did not have any idea of how to run a business and it only lasted for six months before he closed it down. The underground tanks were removed. We both went to watch this occur and shed a tear, and now it is a 7-Eleven site.

Now that I was retired, I could do the things that I had promised to do so many years ago. The most important was to spread the word about the Holocaust (Shoah). Trudy and I visited the Sydney and Melbourne Holocaust museums, and gave lectures at both museums; and met up with survivors, some from Dora and Bergen-Belsen, and presented artefacts and memorabilia to them. I extended my visits to public and private high schools in Brisbane and the Gold Coast Primary School. Students did not seem to be very interested, but I received a standing ovation from the students and teachers at the secondary schools. With the highest of reviews and questions, it was all worth the time.

The highlight was in 1982 when I presented the first Holocaust exhibition in the Brisbane City Hall, under the patronship of the Queensland Premier Sir Joh Bjelke Peterson. It was not very difficult to organize this event because the Premier was a close acquaintance of George Herscu, who came from Oradea and went to school with me. He was a multimillionaire developer who was the owner of LJ Hooker, a very large residential and commercial real estate agency and major shopping centre developer, the same as Frank Lowy and John Saunders, both Hungarian Jews, who own the Westfield Group. George Herscu wanted to develop and build four large shopping centres at Sunnybank, a suburb of Brisbane. He wanted development application approved from the Queensland government to build an overhead pedestrian bridge over a main road to adjoin two of his shopping centres. He gave a bribe under the table in a plain paper bag to the Premier. The project was approved immediately, of course. The overhead bridge still stands today. An inquiry was set up and George Herscu was found to be guilty and promptly incarcerated.

Trudy came to the rescue again. She cooked and delivered kosher food to him in prison. He was eventually paroled and I went guarantor for him. It was the least I could do for him, as he spoke to the Premier about the Holocaust Exhibition. On his release he came and stayed with us for a while then went to America to join his son, and a while later died a very rich man.

Now back to the Holocaust Exhibition. It was also patronised by Sir Zelman Cowan, the Jewish former Governor-General of Australia. I was assisted by my very old best friend George Fry, who was a tailor. He made replica striped pyjama suits with a yellow star with the word 'JUDE' embroidered on it, depicting the clothes we wore during the Holocaust. It bought back nightmares. The exhibition was very successful and achieved the ultimate goal of opening people's eyes and to "Remember and never forget". My ultimate goal is to one day establish a modern permanent museum in Brisbane, the same as Sydney and Melbourne. Hopefully this will happen in my lifetime.

I authored a large manuscript which I donated to the Queensland Museum with other items including a havdalah candle (a three-wick candle symbolising the three stars that is used on Sabbath) and a menorah that I made at home in my workshop using my lathe. I did radio interviews, mainly at 4BC with my old friends Hyden Sargent and Greg Cary, whose stepfather survived the Holocaust. I did several articles for the *Australian Jewish*

News, and *The Courier-Mail* and various TV interviews
when the need arose. Also did the DVD documentary
about Dora, BBC, German and Canadian TV. It occupied
my time and I enjoyed it.

Dora-Mittlebau

In 1989, after the unification of East and West Germany,
Dora was handed back to the new German Democratic
Republic government. The tunnels were re-opened and
a new state-of-the-art modern museum was built and
established. I was invited and attended the first memorial
service after the opening as one of the survivors of the
famous three hundred selected by VW Works at Auschwitz.

This service was held on the 17th April 1990. I attended
with Trudy of course, we went every year together. It was
a solemn occasion. There I met the new young director,
Professor Dr Jens Christian Wagner, who was doing his
thesis. We became the best of friends and remained so for
many years to come. I wrote many letters to him about
the Shoah (Holocaust). When we visited, we would always
take along two bottles of Australian Grange Hermitage
wine as a present. My son Michael did the same when he
and his wife visited in 2014. The biggest highlight was to
be interviewed in the award-winning documentary DVD,
written and produced by Dr Wagner, *Dora – Concentration
Camp of the "Total War".* Also appearing was Simon Hersh
Z"L from Sydney. I was interviewed on my last ever visit
by Professor Dr Karsten Uhl, the present director of Dora.

Dr Wagner has been promoted and is now in charge of all museums in Germany. The last time I visited was in 2010 by myself, and on that occasion – the reason will become evident – I was honoured with presenting a speech at the service and acting as the official guide.

Another great honour is that my photo is displayed at the entrance of the museum and is still there on display. I have only visited Bergen-Belsen (the living death camp) once, and will never go again because of the pain, and I have never and will never go to Auschwitz-Birkenau. I refuse to, in memory of my late father Mikosh, mother Helena, and sister Anita.

CHAPTER 23

Gertrude (Trudy) Stein, the Love Of My Life. The Final Chapter.

My other great passion in life was the South Brisbane Synagogue. Trudy and I continued going. There was a change of president at the synagogue and the original rabbi moved on. I do not know if is a Jewish thing that there has to be bickering, arguing and petty politics involved. I have always stayed clear of those things and ignored them. Life is too short, and I am too busy doing other things to get involved. Anyway I was not shattered by those events. I could devote more time to the Holocaust cause. Trudy took it another way and has never, ever been back, or ever will go there again. She was very strong-willed in her ways. I became the stand-in rabbi and happily attended. People admired me for that.

Many years later, at the 100th anniversary of the South Brisbane Hebrew congregation celebrations, a stained-glass portrait of me was commissioned and hangs proudly in the synagogue.

The Final Chapter

Trudy's health started to deteriorate in mid-2005. While she was shopping with Dulcie Townsend, she had a dizzy spell and blacked out. The warning signs had appeared, rearing their ugly head. Maybe it was due to the 80 Camel Regular Non Filter cigarettes she smoked per day. It is a European thing. I was also a heavy smoker once but gave up, and all of Trudy's family were also heavy smokers. Her father died of throat cancer. All of my children except for Frank and Benny also smoke. Dulcie sat her down and she recovered and told Dulcie that she was ok.

The last trip we did together was in mid-December 2006, to the northern rivers of New South Wales, and we had a beautiful picnic on top of a hill overlooking magnificent countryside. Once again she had a turn. On returning home we visited our local doctor Dr Ian Sunderland, and his wife Betty, who was also a doctor. We are the best of friends from old Zillmere days. He admitted her immediately to the Holy Spirit Northside Private Hospital at Chermside, and she was diagnosed with stage 4 lung cancer, with only a short time to live. Frank and Benny both flew home from Israel straight away. I took a bottle of Dom Pérignon Champagne to her on new year's eve and the whole family celebrated with Trudy at her bedside. I did not care what the doctors or others thought. They better had not said anything or otherwise there would be serious consequences from a upset angry Romanian. Anyway we cheered the new year in and for all of us to have a final drink with her. Trudy and I were not drinkers so she made the effort to have two sips. The specialists and doctors said for me to take her home as there was no more that could be done.

We made her as comfortable as possible, spending most of the days lying on a sunchair on the terrazzo-floored balcony with all her indoor plants as always. She did not complain. We all knew that she was in terrible pain. We supplied her with medical oxygen to help her breathe. Finally we had to move her to our bed of so many years. Dr Sutherland gave prescriptions for high dose morphine, which Reuben administered.

Gertrude 'Trudy' Stein passed away at 6 pm on the 29th January 2006 surrounded by all her children at her bedside. Trudy always said that she would only leave 28 Fernlea Street, Geebung, in a coffin – and she did.

The Funeral

The funeral was held at the Jewish Chapel, Mt Gravatt Cemetery, the chapel that I built as president of the Brisbane Chevra Kadisha. It was and still is a blur. I was too upset to conduct the service. I remember reading out Psalm 26 ('The Lord Is my Shepherd') in Hebrew and English. I sat with my children and grandchildren and sobbed with tears uncontrollably, which I have done so many times before, and I cuddled Michael. Trudy lies next to the Holocaust memorial that I also erected in honour of my father Mikosh, my mother Helena, and my older sister Anita. It was the biggest funeral ever held at this chapel. It was packed. There was standing room only, with people standing at both sides and at the rear. We then moved on to the gravesite and recited the Kiddush, the Jewish Prayer for Mourning the Departed. We also sat Shiva for three days at home with the whole family. Once again it was packed.

Gertrude Trude Stein Z"L. A woman of worth.

CHAPTER 24

The Aftermath.
After George Moshe Stein.

I was in a weird state after Trudy's funeral. Frank and Benny went back to Israel. Reuben was still living at home. All I wanted to do is mourn for Trudy and think about all the good times that we had, and the bad ones. For example, for over 60 years she cleaned the house and kept it in an immaculate condition, and have to put up with my moods when I was at home. One day, when I was in one of those moods, I said to her, "Why don't you feed me better food and look after me better?"

She exploded and said "OK. I am not going to cook for you for two weeks", and she kept her promise. I had to go to McDonalds, have fish and chips, or go to the Kedron-Wavell RSL Club. It was the worst experience of my life. I should have known better than to upset her. Also during those two weeks, we had no contact and I had to sleep downstairs in the workshop or in the car, and also she did not speak to me. The only time was to yell at me and tell me to pick up my rubbish and clothes, and to put away my shoes that I had left behind. I also had to do my own washing. Things did improve but I knew that I had to watch my step and temper.

One pasttime that we did enjoy together after I retired, was to go and have a little punt at the Kedron-Wavell RSL Club. I first went there with Michael on his first leave after he returned from being overseas in 1968, but stayed away until I retired. We used to go on a Sunday night for the members jackpot draw, but we never won. The staff there used to call her Gertie, and occasionally we used to go to the casino in Brisbane or the Gold Coast.

As I stated, I became lost and all that I wanted to do and did was to become recluse and hibernate. Reuben and I had a major falling out and he went and lived by himself. Hannah visited regularly as she had just separated from her husband. I also curtailed my communal duties and activities and resigned from the Zionist Federation of Queensland, but still remained president of the Brisbane Chevra Kadisha since we were very busy, as people were passing at a very high rate because of the aging local Jewish community. I continued, but at a lesser pace, with my Holocaust lectures to schools. I only visited the Dora memorial service once after Trudy passed, but I still remained in touch and communicated by writing letters to my old friend Dr Wagner.

Life had changed dramatically. I spent a lot of my time with my old friend George Frey, who also had lost his wife Fay. We go and have Sunday breakfast at the RSL Club. The community put on a special function and dinner, which was packed of course, attended by both of our families. It was called the Two Georges. We also went on two South Pacific Cruises with the Holland-American shipping line.

I still attended the synagogue for many years and also drove my little VW Polo, which was given to me by VW Works Head Office as restitution for the atrocities at Dora (I should not talk about that because I had signed a confidentiality agreement many years ago, along with the life pension, after the class action taken out in America). I became my own chief cook and bottle washer, went shopping at Aldi every week and did the cooking – sort of.

Then in March 2009, it happened again. As mentioned previously, my son Frank passed. I then went downhill rapidly. Benny calls me every Saturday night and he keeps me informed about my granddaughters. He visits each year and I have visited only once, and bought a piano for his daughters. He also visited once with his children. I have always had problems with my knees, and had a double knee construction in about 1990 or so while Trudy was here to look after me. My knees went again and I had them done again at Greenslopes Private Hospital by a Jewish orthopaedic surgeon that I know. All on my own this time. My children came to visit regularly. It was very painful. I stayed in hospital for four weeks, and then came home and had intensive care from St Luke's Nursing Service.

As I stated, I had lost all interest, especially in the house. Reuben comes over and does the yard and removes all of the rubbish. Also the front stairs collapsed. I submitted an insurance claim, but it was rejected because the damage was caused by termites. I had paid thousands to have a termite barrier installed but it had failed. The stairs were condemned and I had to replace them and install a new termite barrier. In January 2011, Michael had his 60th birthday and invited me along. I attended and was very happy because the communication is there now. After many years he does not visit very often because of work commitments and the distance, it takes about an hour to come and see me. My children also took me to coffee at the Coffee Club, and at one time we all went for lunch at The Full Moon Hotel at Sandgate. It used to be our favourite place. We would sit outside and happily reflect on the past and gaze at the ocean and see Bribie Island. The happy times came back. But on this occasion, I put my foot in it. I observed a waiter throwing out a piece of bread into a bin. I completely lost it, as at Dora bread was so precious, we only received one slice a day – that was all that we got fed for the day. It is sacred. I told him what I thought and let him have it.

I was getting old and weary. I knew it but did not want to realize it. My driving became erratic to everyone else but me. I have driven army trucks at night in the dark without any lights on the winding mountainous gravel roads at Admont, which was no easy task. What happened is that while parking in the disabled park at the RSL, I smashed into the barrier and nearly collided with the front door. The police came and informed me that I had to sit a driver's test. I did but failed, and of course argued with the driving instructor, and told him that he did not know what he was talking about. My licence was cancelled immediately for life. Life became very difficult without a car. I sold my little VW. Reuben and Hannah took me shopping every week. Reuben took me to the synagogue, and when he was not available I caught a bus into the city, and the president of the South Brisbane Synagogue would pick me up and take me back to the city, and I caught the bus home.

One day, while making a cup of coffee, I burnt my hand and dropped the kettle. I decided that I would go and buy a new one at Kmart. While walking along the highway on Gympie Road, with the said kettle in hand, I was picked up by the police and taken to the Prince Charles Hospital at Chermside. I was admitted and assessed and stayed there for two weeks, then transferred to Eventide assessment centre at Sandgate and stayed there for three weeks; then sent home with daily visits from Health Department nurses to keep an eye on me. Reuben visited daily and made sure I was taking my insulin. I was a mess. I became incontinent, and I knew then that I was on the way out.

I called Reuben and he took me straight away to the Regis Sandgate aged care centre.

That is all from me, George Stein. I had a good life. I want to go and to be with Trudy.

Goodbye,

George

CHAPTER 25

Life of George Moshe Stein.

Michael Stein

Where do I start? I am Michael, the son of George and Gertrude Stein. What a story! How can I follow that. It is all true. Dad was taken to Regis Sandgate aged care centre by my brother Reuben. Dad was not able to take care of himself any longer and, putting it mildly, he had had enough. He was tired and could not cope any more, especially after losing Mum and Frank, and all of what he had been through over the last 80 years or so, as you would have read earlier in this book. To see such a vibrant, energetic *mensch* become so frail was a sad sight. He did so much for the community and spread the word to the world about the Holocaust, and not to see his dream of establishing a museum being established in Queensland come to fruition is soul breaking – but it has happened and the museum is now here.

On with the story. In July 2021, Dad was first put into the general ward at Musgrave House. Reuben did a sterling job with all that he has done. Hannah, my wife Karen and I went to see him at least three times a week. Dad had advanced dementia and gangrene of the feet caused by diabetes.

One story I must tell is: we received a phone call one night – one of many – informing us that Dad had absconded. It is not known how he did it, as he was on the second floor with no exit and all the doors locked and guarded by staff. I went and visited Dad with Marco the manager, and I asked Dad, "Did you go for an adventure?"

He replied, "No, not me". We looked in his closet and found a plastic bag containing a toothbrush, comb, underwear, t-shirt and shorts, and also remotes for the TV and air conditioning.

This became a regular occurrence and happened at least five times. They would contact the police and inform them, and they would say "Not George again" and the staff would reply "Yes, George again". Through all his time at Regis, Dad would mumble in strange languages and no one could understand him. Dad spoke five languages fluently.

He ended up having five or so falls and always ended up at Redcliffe Hospital. Eventually he was transferred to Griffith House, a specialised secure dementia building. It was self-contained and modern, with an on-site and television. He enjoyed watching the Food Channel. Dad loved it there. We hung family photos and a large photo of Mum, but he pulled them down and I had to secure them. The highlight was going and having morning tea with him, especially on Saturdays. He would always ask for two pieces of cake. His hunger never waned. We had to have a coffee with him, and I took sips out of an empty cup. We used to take him for walks and as he sat on a bench we asked him, "What you are doing?"

The answer was "I am waiting for the bus to take me to Bribie", where their holiday house was, or town for the fireworks, or the seniors concert.

Things did deteriorate very quickly. He was rushed to Redcliffe Hospital, and operated on immediately for his foot. He had two operations and the doctors were worried about his age. I was there when he woke up from the second operation. They dressed him in a hospital gown and when he woke up he thought he was back at Bergen-Belsen again – they dressed the prisoners in similar gowns. Dad went ballistic and pulled out the drips and had to be held down by four staff members. Finally he settled down. The specialists advised that the best thing to do was to send him back to Griffith on end-of-life care. Benny came from Israel, and he had visits from the rabbi.

On our last visit Dad was lying in bed trying to watch the Food Channel, and was in pain and heavily sedated. Karen was lying with him as he hugged her. Dad loved Karen very much. He held her hand and said "I do not want to go yet as I have more to say and do". He then looked at me with a smile and said "Go to Dora for me and say goodbye". I said and did.

I went in April this year for the memorial service and stood next to Dad's old mate Dr Wagner. I took an Australian flag and presented it to the museum along with two bottles of wine. They put on a memorial lunch for Dad on the 15th April 2023 at noon, at the exact same time that Dad passed.

George Moshe Stein passed at 8:30 on the 15th April 2022, the same time that Dora was liberated by the American Fourth Army.

The funeral was held at the Mt Gravatt Jewish section. The service was held in the chapel that Dad built so many years ago. There was a large crowd in attendance. The service was conducted by the South Brisbane Synagogue in honour of Dad. A special eulogy was sent and read by Dr Wagner, and the 26th was read in Hebrew and English, the same as it was for Mum's funeral. Dad now lies with his darling Trudy again next to the Holocaust memorial for his father Mikosh, mother Helen and his sister Anita.

TRIBUTE FROM A GRANDSON

Nick Stein

So, I don't usually get this personal, but this week Brisbane/ the world lost one of the last holocaust survivors: my grandpa, George Stein, 95.

He was a flawed individual for those that knew him best, yet that could be explained through the pure horrors he survived. He firstly survived Auschwitz where he last saw his mother, father and sister, who all perished at the camp. Then spent years in the Dora concentration camp before being sent to Bergen-Belsen until he was liberated. He survived the worst of humanity yet went about starting a family and a life including my father and four other uncles and aunties. He passed away almost 77 years to the day of his liberation at Bergen-Belsen. As one of my uncles put it best, he got his revenge on the Nazis by surviving to live to 95 years, starting a successful business and raising a family, including five grandkids. What he went through needs to be understood by all, so it never happens again.

George Moshe Stein Z"L

1.2.1927 – 15.4 2022

"Good can always come from adversity."

"Dora. What a beautiful name a girls name. How can such a beautiful place be the scene of such atrocities."
– George Moshe Stein.

"He was a worried soul, (to brave to admit it, and this he had to live with) of strong heart and will, but he would never let the Nazi bastards win."
– Michael Stein.

CHAPTER 26

Life of Michael Stein.

Michael Stein

I am George Stein's son. He is my hero. We are so similar in every way. We fight, we argue, but we have gone through the same things, with many tears and heart breaks, but the main fact will always remain that we love each other.

But there are differences between us. Dad's father was very religious, a trait that Dad followed to the letter. I admire him for that. He forced his thoughts on religion in a very committed manner, especially to Reuben and me. Of course, we had our own beliefs and acted accordingly when we left home. I believed, but not as an orthodox Jew, as I had my own plans for the future. Dad did relax this stipulation to his other children.

I was born at Bat Yam, Tel Aviv on the 20th January 1951. Life was good. I had my tricycle with an Israeli flag on it. I played with my brother Reuben and with Rivka and Fenya, two girls who were our neighbours.

My mother Gertrude used to take us down to the beach. Because of his horrific past life, he was very strict in all ways. He never forgave or forgot about anything and had a very hard, tough appearance. It was difficult for him to show compassion and affection (this is a common thread for Holocaust survivors), especially to Reuben and me. I never remember being hugged or being praised. I rang Dad every week, but he was dazed or did not care. I do not know. I know it is common with Holocaust survivors. I was watching a documentary on television about Betty Klimenko, the principal of Erebus Motorsport, whose stepfather was a Holocaust survivor from Hungary. Jeno Schwarcz was his name – he changed it to John Saunders. He was the founding partner of Westfield, along with Frank Lowy. She stated that she also rang her stepfather each week and that there was silence on the other end, but she knew he was there. She kept calling. One day he answered and spoke to her. Deep down I know that he wanted to.

Another example is that of Michael Gudinski Z"L, the founder of Mushroom Records and Frontier Touring Company. His father came from Russia and he wanted Michael to choose a different career path and their relation became strained.

But in my case Mum was there to show and give affection, and that made up for it.

Dad was very humble and never asked for appreciation praise for whatever he did. I remember in 1990, he was offered an Order of Australia medal, but he declined. His reasoning was "I do not deserve it".

At the age of six, we all came to Australia. I did not want to go, but upon arrival things quickly changed. We stayed with our grandparents who spoiled us rotten. Australia is my country and always will be. I do not have any special love for Israel like Dad did, even though I was born there. Both Karen and I have been back and visited on one of our trips. We were walking through a supermarket with Frank. He and I were in deep conversation when we hear loud shouting and yelling in Hebrew. We turned around and to my astonishment there was an armed security guard with his rifle aimed at Karen's face. Frank took action immediately and the situation came to an end. Apparently, he asked Karen something, she did not understand because she does not speak Hebrew. That was enough for me. I had an important task to accomplish and that was to deliver documentation to Yad Vashem in Jerusalem about Dad's father Mikosh, mother Helena, and older sister Anita, to be deposited in their vast library. Karen and I did this task. What an emotional place to visit. I did not want to be involved in a place where people are subject to this kind of treatment and live in fear of war. When I was young, all I heard about was Israel was a poor country and needed financial assistance from Jews worldwide, but in reality it is not poor at all, with wealth apparent everywhere.

I went back only once and visited Frank's grave in Jerusalem, with his best mate David Hersch. We said

Kiddush together. Frank was very special. 'Farmer Fred'
I used to call him because he used to wear Jed Clampet
overalls. Always before he came to visit each August to go
to the Brisbane Exhibition, he would call Karen and asked
her how many bottles of Estée Lauder white linen did she
have left, and he would bring various amounts from Hong
Kong, also a supply of moisturiser and other cosmetics
from the Dead Sea. I did not miss out because there was
always a bottle of Sabra liquor. We miss Farmer Fred. It
has been fourteen years since his passing.

During the Holocaust, a lot of Jewish people escaped
including Dad's relatives, his uncle who attended Hannah's
wedding, and a young boy named Rick who fled to Britian.
His name is Rick Stein, the world-famous Michelin Star
chef. If you see his photo, he is the spitting image of Frank.

Life was very tough when we first came to Zillmere.
I was bullied at school. No matter how poor we were,
Mum sent Reuben and I to school with salami sandwiches
and shoes and socks. All the other kids wore thongs. We
were different and my father was a rich Jew who owned
the service station. One afternoon whilst walking home
we were bashed up and our shoes and socks were thrown
away, and we were thrown in to the creek next to the
railway line. But I got over it, that is life. We went to
primary school at Zillmere State School. I remember
a girl by the name of Marcia Langton – a First Nation
person, well known for her reconciliation activities. My
best friend then was a person by the name of Graham

Hutchinson. I remember that I was very excited when I got invited to his birthday party. He did very well in life, a music promoter and he was responsible for bringing out the Russian and Bolshoi Ballet in later years. I have never caught up with him again. I went to high school at Aspley State High School.

At 16 I wanted to spread my wings and explore this wide, exciting world. I did. School life and study was not for me, and I joined the Royal Australia Navy for twelve years, sent to the junior recruit training establishment HMAS *Leeuwin* at Fremantle, Western Australia. It was tough. I was bullied, assaulted, vilified with antisemitism because I was of a different religion. One example was something called 'running the gauntlet', where a pillowcase is put over your head and you are made to run along a corridor with senior recruits armed with irons stuffed in pillowcases hitting you as you run. Discrimination is still rife in the services as can be witnessed in the finding of many inquiries and Royal Commissions. It would be too horrific to explain what I went through in those early years as a junior recruit. And the mental health issues and suicides that occur by ex-service people. I remember one Anzac Day, after the service in Townsville, a veteran of Iraq and Afghanistan took his own life that afternoon. I overcame all of this. It was a good lesson in life. I saw active service overseas and served on HMAS *Vendetta* (three times), HMAS *Stuart* (Royal tour 1970) HMAS *Duchess*, and HMAS *Vampire* Coxswain (regulating Branch Naval Police).

I married a Sydney girl and had a daughter, Rachel, who died of SIDS aged six months and two days old. I finished my service as a Petty Officer Coxswain. I resigned from the services moved to Brisbane and bought a house. I went to work with Dad – which did not work out – and had another daughter Rebecca in 1977. My first wife went back to her parents with my daughter. That was 45 years ago and have not seen her since. After leaving Dad's business I had several jobs and my own business with an annual turnover of $450,000. I married my present wife in 1986 and am happily married with two dogs. I am retired and have dramas like everyone with the likes of Telstra, Foxtel, Centrelink and the Department of Veterans' Affairs. I am an active member of the Returned Services League and a dedicated fan of the Cowboys Rugby League team and the Brisbane Lions AFL team.

It was very difficult for Dad when Mum passed. I tried to get close but could not visit because there were too many memories at Geebung, of my childhood and later years. Since then I have not gone there very often. We used to take Dad to lunch once at a special place, the Full Moon Hotel at Sandgate. It was Mum's favourite place, sitting on the hill overlooking the ocean and with Bribie Island in the distance. Also we used to go to breakfast at Kedron-Wavell services club, and Dad did attend my 60th birthday celebration along with all the family. He give me a heartful card, so he really is soft-hearted.

A very emotional trip we did in 2014 was to find Dad's

house at Oradea to give final closure. We told Dad and he was full of anticipation. He gave us the address and a map of the location. It was exact, and we told him also that we would visit Dora. He said do not forget the two bottles of Grange Hermitage wine for Dr Wagner – it was mandatory, Dad said. So off we went. We hired a turbo Audi SUV from Avis at Frankfurt Airport and did the three-hour trip to Nordhausen on the Autobahn at 200 kilometres an hour. We arrived and presented our gift to Dr Wagner and were welcomed with a warm affectionate hug, and then the mandatory cup of coffee and a long chat. Dr Wagner said that he misses Dad, and his last visit was in 2010. I explained Dad's emotional state of mind.

Then the best was to come. We were given a personal guided tour of the tunnel, which was very rare as only group tours were permitted. I found out later that personal tours were only reserved for special heads of state and VIPs, for example, the Queen and Duke of Edinburgh on their tour of Germany. The tunnel was a solemn moving experience. It was as if nothing had changed. The smell, the array of half-assembled V-2 rockets lying among the subterranean underground lake, with unknown remains of imprisoned forced labour prisoners. We were shown Dad's work bench standing there as a memorial in the same condition as it was so many years ago. The only difference was that a plaque had been erected on it bearing 'George Moshe Stein'.

We then did a walkaround of the state-of-the-art

museum and, as soon as you walk in, their first framed photo is that of Dad at the reopening of the site in 1990. We bade our farewell to Dr Wagner.

The next morning, we started our exciting re-enactment as Dad did so many years ago. We did not stop at Bergen-Belsen or Auschwitz Buchenwald out of respect for Dad and his parents and sister. We stopped and played tourists at Leipzig, Prague, Bratislava and Budapest. We then travelled to the Hungarian–Romanian border. We only had ten kilometres to travel. We were full of anticipation. On arrival we were stopped by armed guards (Romania is still under Soviet control) who asked us: "Who are you? Where are you from? Where are you going to? And where did you steal the car from?"

I answered, "We are from Australia. We are going to find my father's house from the Holocaust". They held us for an hour and a half and came back and said that I had a Romanian face, and that I got the car Avis at Frankfurt Airport. They then now stated, "You can go. Computer kaput".

We arrived at Oradea. The town seemed to be in a time warp from the '40s, with old grand buildings. The only form of modernisation were the trams, and fast internet speeds (we could learn a lesson from them), and a large array of poker machines. We checked in to the hotel and from the top floor of our suite we looked out at my father's birth town. With directions and, map in hand, I asked the manager "How in the bloody hell do we find this joint?

He said, "No worries, it is easy. In the morning, go down the main street and you will see old fellows sitting down drinking coffee and smoking. Show them the map and ask directions".

The next morning, we walked down there and at the first table there were four people sitting there. We showed them the map and photo. One fellow said "Follow me", and then like many years ago, I walked down the cobblestone street and stopped at a building and he pointed here. We found it.

The door to the building was open we walked in as so many years ago. I knocked on the door and there was no answer. We went back to the hotel and had a drink and decided to go back later, which we did. This time success. A young couple opened the door, and I explained the situation. They welcomed us in and showed us around. I took photos and immediately rang Dad. He was elated, and you could feel the happiness and tears. Mission accomplished. But this time Dad was not heart-broken. We had successfully retraced his adventure. It felt good. We visited the synagogue where the family prayed. It was being rebuilt. We also went to his school where he played so long ago. The adventure was not completed, we went back to Budapest, and then on to Admont. Dad was not wrong: the road was nothing but 20 kilometres steep winding mountain roads. We stayed in a medieval castle/Schloss hotel on top of the town.

The next morning went and saw the Admont

Displacement Camp in a beautiful valley in the Austrian alps. There are townhouses there now but the front gate still stands as a memorial. Also there is a memorial centre which we visited and saw a photo of Dad standing in front of an army truck and another photo of Dad with his soccer team. Next to this centre was a dance school with the name of Kager Dance, Mum's maiden name. Our next stop was the town of Maribor in Slovenia, where Mum was born, and stayed at a ski resort there. As we were leaving Maribor and were stopped at traffic lights, I saw a sign and a big warehouse, Harvey Norman Maribor. There was not much to see there, and finally to Salzburg where Mum also grew up.

Two days before Dad passed, Karen and I visited Dad. He was watching the Food Channel. He was in pain and highly sedated. Karen was beside him giving him a hug. Dad loved Karen. He looked her in the eyes yet and said "I do not want to go yet, there is a lot more to tell". He looked at me and said "Michael, go back to Dora for me and say farewell". I promised him that I would.

I visited Dora on the 15th April this year for the 78th anniversary service of Liberation. I was greeted by Professor Dr Karsten Uhl, the present director of the Dora Museum and had the pleasure of sitting with Dr Wagner. I took the customary two bottles of wine. There were only three survivors in attendance. One of the survivors from America was at Dora when he was 17 with his father who died there. He attended with his children and they

Michael Stein with Prof Dr Jens Christan Wagner at the 78th memorial service, 15th April 2023, held at Dora, Nordhausen.

held a memorial service at the crematorium and recited Kiddush. It was very moving. I was given an Australian flag by Milton Dick, the local federal member of parliament, who knew Dad, which had been flown at Parliament House, Canberra. I was given a memorial attended by one hundred people in honour of Dad at the same time one year after Dad passed. This is the same date that in 1945 that the United States Fourth Army Division liberated Dora.

We must remember all profits of this book are going to be donated to the Queensland Holocaust Museum.

To my late father George Moshe Stein, your courage in

adversity and strong will and never give up.

Dad's dream has now come to fruition: the establishment of a Holocaust Museum in Brisbane. Please buy this book and visit the museum.

How could a person endure so many heartbreaks, tears and have the will to achieve his hopes and aspirations? This is the most harrowing experience of my life, reading the manuscripts and documentation so carefully written by my late father. The title is so true: Good Will Always Come From Adversity.

Michael Stein
mkstein@bigpond.com

Siblings.

You would all have heard of the television series *Succession*; anybody would think that Dad was the author. He never forgave or forgot. The consequences that occurred to my brothers and sister and myself after his passing.

For example, Dad had ten wills with the Queensland Public Trustee. Every time he had issues with any of us he would change his will, and he was the master of playing one of us against the other, which of course led to an unresolvable relationship with us. Maybe one day this can be mended. It tears me apart and I know Mum would be sorting him out in the way she always did.

He is at peace with his Dad, Mum and sister, along with Trudy and Frank. I can visualise the heated discussions with John Lipski, Morris Orchard, George Hersch, and a multitude of other people.

ACHIEVEMENTS OF GEORGE STEIN

To say that Dad stayed still was inarguable. This is a list of his achievements:

- Founding Member Zillmere Chamber of Commerce
- Foundation Member Rotary Club of Geebung (Paul Harris Fellow)
- Foundation President B'nai B'rith Queensland
- President Queensland Jewish Board of Deputies
- Queensland President Zionist Federation of Australia.
- President Chevra Kadisha (Jewish Burial Society)
- Queensland Jewish Ex Serviceman's Association
- Vice President Jewish Communal Centre
- President South Brisbane Synagogue
- Yearly visits to Dora Museum Nordhausen, to commemorate the reembrace of Liberation 11–16 April
- Construction, financing of the new South Brisbane synagogue (brick by brick) and purchasing land and house for accommodation for the rabbi and building of a Mikvah (Jewish female cleansing bath)
- Holding the first Queensland Holocaust Exhibition at the Brisbane City Hall in 1982, under the patronship of Sir Joh Bjelke Peterson, Queensland Premier, and Sir Zelman Cowan, Governor General
- Lectures about the Holocaust to schools and colleges and many organizations and clubs

- Interviews and Documentaries including *"Dora – Concentration Camp of the 'Total War'"* DVD 12014. Interviews with BBC, Canadian German TV, radio interviews on 4BC Brisbane, ABC, newspaper articles *Courier Mail, Sunday Mail, Australian Jewish News* and J wire.

ACKNOWLEDGEMENTS

What a challenge putting to paper the words of passed loved ones, and going through the trials and tribulations you have to stay strong gratitude has guided me through life's long and winding road, Dad you were a worried soul, but you never let the Nazi bastards win.

To my late mother Gertrude (Trudy) Stein thank you for your support shoulder to lean on, guidance, sympathy, and discipline you were truly a woman of worth.

My long-suffering wife of 39 years, Karen, the only person who could control me. I do not know how you could put up with me. Thank you.

Professor Dr Jens Christan Wagner for being there for my father after he lost the love of his life, and listening to him while he was in a lost world of darkness.

Morrie Singer Z"L who was there to liberate my father and others from Bergen-Belsen (The living hell) so many years ago Morrie Singer's son Peter, and also a special thank you to David Hersh (whose father Simon Hersh Z"L was at Dora with Dad) both of you were there to show and give for their love and support of their best mate and my late brother Frank Stein Z"L.

Marcus Fielding managing Director of Echo Books for all your guidance and the motivation to keep on writing. A special thank you and appreciation to Jason Steinberg for his never-ending motivation and success in establishing the Queensland Holocaust Museum, a dream that my father never saw come to fruition (we must remember and never forget).

Thank you to the one and only Greg Cary, who gave me the inspiration to write this book. Please buy his book *An Absence Of Certainty* and you will understand what a caring person he is.

Thank you to Jim Chalmers MP for listening and driving the funding for the Queensland Holocaust Museum.

The Holocaust Mark Two.

7.10.2024

In the early morning of the 7th October 2023. Hamas terrorists invaded the Super Nova Festival in the southern Gaza Strip. This event was attended by thousands of young Jewish people who were enjoying their democratic rights to be there. The terrorists paraglided and broke the secure surround of this festival, and murdered hundreds of people, raped females, and took over 250 hostages. They also invaded local Kibbitzes and settlements, where they murdered, raped, and beheaded young babies in front of their parents, and also killed whole families and took more hostages.

As an Israeli born, I find these occurrences horrific and bring back memories of what happened to my late father George Stein his father Mikosh, Mother Helena, and sister Anita so many years ago. This event has shaken the Jewish people and others here in Australia and worldwide, a feeling of despair and loss is evident. I am usually used to dealing with grief from my many years of service life, but this is very difficult to come to terms with.

The Israeli Army, Navy and Air Force have been put into immediate action and are very swift in their efforts to rescue hostages, and starting to retrieve, identify, and bury my fellow Jewish and non-Jewish victims who came from all nations.

Innocent Palestinians also were and are suffering by the hands of Hamas, by being used as human hostages and are suffering by the retaliation of the Israeli forces which is justified, with the loss of homes, power, water, fuel and hospital facilities. Israel has declared war on Hamas and the goal is to eliminate this ruthless, barbaric organisation which it will do with great vigour and tenacity.

But once again there will be losses by all and with over 300,000 full time and reserve troops on active duty, this will be achieved. The free world has condemned this atrocity, but the there are those who sympathise with these murders and are holding rallies and demonstrations worldwide and in Australia. I have a brother Benny who lives in Tel Aviv with his wife and his two daughters Noa, and Tair, they are in their late twenties. We thought that they attended the Super Nova Festival as young people do, but with communication being difficult we were not sure. It has been confirmed that they are safe and have been recalled to the Israeli Army. Undoubtedly, they had friends that have been murdered or are being held hostage.

What has happened is as bad or if not worse than the Holocaust. It makes me more determined to fulfil the promise that I made on my late father's death bed, to educate and inform everyone about the Shoah (Holocaust) and what has happened in Gaza. We must never forget this is the reason that I have written this book in the memory of all that have perished then and now. War is not nice or pretty. I know this first hand.

GOOD CAN ALWAYS COME FROM ADVERSITY
Michael Stein. mkstein@bigpond.com
www.michaelstein.com.au